ANTHOLOGY

Tom MacInnes

ANTHOLOGY

compiled and presented
by Rémi Tremblay

Reconquista Press

© 2021 Reconquista Press
www.reconquistapress.com

ISBN: 978-1-912853-27-4

CONTENTS

About Tom MacInnes 9
Introduction to MacInnes' Poetry 25
    Rubric 33

A. Adventure/Action
    Amber Lands 37
    Laughter 43
    Ballade of the Free Lance 47
    Ballade of Action 48
    Lady of Ventures 49

B. British epics and narratives
    For the Crowning of the King 53
    On Beacon Hill 60
    Fey 67
    The Lost Castle 71

C. Canadian epics and narratives
    Lonesome Bar 75
    The Rhyme of Jacques Valbeau 90
    The Chilcoot Pass 107

D. Youth/Old
    October 115
    Lone Wolf Lament 116
    Forty 118
    Ballade of the Easy Way 120
    The Ballad of Youth Remaining 121
    Villanelle of Mutton 122
    Ballade of Sleep 123

E. Earthly considerations
  - Ballade of Detachment ... 127
  - The Tiger of Desire ... 128
  - The Modernists ... 129
  - Dreamers in Romance ... 130
  - Always Trouble ... 130
  - What Answer? ... 131
  - The Master Profiteers ... 132
  - Plotted Not for Profit ... 132
  - The Odd Impulse to Serve ... 133

F. Love and other pleasures
  - Mirelle of Found Money ... 137
  - Mirelle of the Good Bed ... 138
  - Love ... 139
  - Among the Queers ... 139
  - Zalinka ... 140

G. Nature
  - Yolana ... 145
  - Indian Summer Beauty ... 147
  - Good-Bye ... 148

H. Death
  - The Tomb ... 151
  - The Isles of Gold ... 152
  - Ballade of Waiting ... 153
  - With the Seven Sleepers ... 154
  - Ballade of the Picaroon ... 155
  - Wan Angel over Me ... 156
  - Wondrous Anodyne! ... 156

I. Religion
  - Content ... 159
  - Nirvana ... 160
  - The Gentle Knave ... 161
  - Infidel ... 162

Bibliography ... 163

ABOUT TOM MACINNES

Nowadays, the name of Tom MacInnes may not ring a bell to most Canadians or even literature enthusiasts, but a century ago, he was among the most popular poets above the 49th parallel. An original author, he was among the pioneers of a genuine Canadian literature. Why was he forgotten then? The most probable answer must be a general amnesia fueled by an education system that has replaced classics with ethnic productions. Very few Canadians could actually name one local author from the beginning of the 20th century. This is how much Canadian culture has declined.

Another reason why MacInnes' memory was blackballed is because of his politically incorrect stance, his views being not so far from those held by Jack London, an Asian-exclusionist Socialist or Rudyard Kipling, famous for his "white man's burden" belief, or even Joseph Conrad, the British imperialist. MacInnes' lack of present-day recognition may have saved him the book burning and statue smashing currently trending in North America, but this great poet deserves better than oblivion, hence this short anthology designed to counter the "erasure," to use Orwell's term, that plagues his legacy.

Tom MacInnes was born into a wealthy Scottish family on October 29, 1867, the very same year the Confederation Act was signed, making Canada an official Dominion, on the path to becoming a nation. He was born in the small city of Dresden, Ontario, and was christened Thomas Robert Edward McInnes. Only much later in life, would he become known as Tom

MacInnes, altering the spelling of his last name for reasons unknown[1].

When Tom was only seven, his father, Thomas Robert McInnes, a respected physician who had served in the Union army, moved the family West to British Columbia, which had joined Confederation three years earlier. In fact, as Tom put it, the family arrived in this still wild province along with the first pioneers. Of those, Tom would later say to express his respect and admiration that "there was a certain seriousness and personal dignity, even among the most common of them, which was characteristic of all our pioneers to the end of the last century; a seriousness and dignity enhanced by living so much alone in forests and by the sea."

Thomas McInnes senior quickly became a respected member of the emerging British Columbian society, becoming mayor of New Westminster in 1877, and Member of Parliament the year after. His involvement in the Grand Lodge of British Columbia probably helped his advancement. In 1881, he was appointed Senator and in 1897, Lieutenant Governor of British Columbia, thus becoming the representative of the Queen of the United Kingdom for the province. His political advancement came to a sudden halt when he was dismissed from his position by the Prime Minister Wilfrid Laurier, something rarely seen in Canada. If Tom took a different path in life than his father, his younger and only brother William would follow the footsteps of his father, espousing politics and serving as a provincial MP and Minister of Education.

---

[1] The name change may have been motivated by the fact that "Mc" is usually the Irish way of writing "son of" while the Scottish way is almost always "Mac." As his heritage was Scottish, he may have used the "Mac" to avoid being thought of as Irish. Another reason might be that he wanted to dissociate himself from his father, well known in the province, to avoid any confusion.

The son of such a respected man, Tom grew up in a certain opulence, being introduced into British Columbia's most prestigious circles. But that did not mean he was anathema to the wild society surrounding him. As he would later write, "New Westminster was unique in having then the authentic atmosphere of the early American West, mingled with the atmosphere of early Victorian England." Indeed, it was a strange mix that he experienced first hand, as he spent his life split between the Catholic Brothers College of New Westminster, prestigious salons and the wild outback where he met the very core of British Columbia's early life: lumberjacks, Natives, adventurers, etc. As he put it, he was at ease with "correct and urbane Europeans of an early Victorian type, with Canadian trappers and miners and pioneers, with the good Indians of Neolithic outlook and habitudes; and with the elusive and everlasting Chinese."

But it was the men who had chosen the harsh life of the Wild West who had his greatest respect. Not only did Tom grow up reading colonial adventure books and tales of courage such as the ones written by Walter Scott, Samuel Coleridge, Rudyard Kipling and John Keats and their ilk, allowing him to dream of these unlikely destinies, but he also developed a passion for the real stories of Captain Jack, Buffalo Bill, Texas Jack, Wild Bill, White Beaver and especially Captain Jack Crawford the Poet Scout, whose lives were at least as exciting as the most imaginative works of fiction. Their long hair, representing a certain form of freedom, inspired his youthful spirit.

The ocean had the same impact on him and aroused his imagination. He could stand on the coast for hours to watch the boats, picturing them "braving uncharted seas and most unfamiliar oceans." If the long hair had his preference, the uniforms of "mariners" certainly came second in his young imagination.

The playground of his youth was the Canadian wilderness, British Columbia's forest and mountains, where he could canoe, fish and trek. All his life, he would go back into this "spirit freeing place," thus preceding Ernst Junger's famous "forest passage."

Like in any "good old days" youth, there was a good deal of magic in his beliefs. He had listened to all the tales and legends about British Columbia's West Coast and most especially about Nootka. Those varied from the sources, might they be British, Indian or Chinese. He then heard that story, among others, of those legendary Buddhist monks who had crossed the Pacific in the year 500 to convert the Natives to their faith. He was also told of these Chinese who came to trade furs as far back as the 18th century. His imagination was bolstered by all the Indian stories about the fairies and spirits living in the endless woods that surrounded him.

The West Coast became his land of reverie.

But, in 1885, at the age where teenagers become known as adults, MacInnes left British Columbia, thus putting an end to his happy, yet adventurous youth.

The timing could not have been better; the age of pioneers was drawing to an end, and as Tom MacInnes left the province to become a man, the province was itself morphing into a civilized society, definitely turning the page on its adventurous infancy.

Tom MacInnes was determined to become a respected man. He studied law at Osgoode Hall Law School Toronto and, in 1889, married Laura Hostetter, a woman coming from a Loyalist family of Niagara. He became a lawyer and started a rather erratic but successful career. He first started to work at official functions in 1896, as a secretary appointed to the Bering Sea Claims Commission to assess damages to be paid by the United States to Canada and Russia for illegal seizure of sealing schooners during the 1880s dispute over sealing rights.

In 1897, while a new Gold Rush was starting in Klondike, he was sent by the government to Skagway to provide provisions and material to the adventurers going North to find the yellow metal, but also to enforce law and avoid smuggling. According to his own recollections, he built the first log cabin of the emerging town, and started playing the piano at night in a dance hall. We can guess that he had found once more the thrill of BC's early days in this manly society.

After having fulfilled this contract, he came back to Vancouver to work as a private secretary to his father, until he officiated as secretary of the British Columbia Salmon Fisheries Commission in 1901.

His career continued forward erratically. In 1908, he was commissioned to act as a counsel for Chinese claimants to assess the damages done in the September 1907 riots. Whites, following the movement started by the Asian Exclusion League, had ransacked the Chinese and Japanese quarters, in a revolt against the "Yellow Peril" that was starting to threaten British Columbia. At that time MacInnes was very admired by the Chinese community whom he highly respected. It is during this mission that he organized a banquet "for better understanding in future between Canadians and the Chinese."

His role had gone even further than establishing links with the Asian community. He had acted as a mole on behalf of Prime Minister Wilfrid Laurier with the Asian Exclusion League and had even helped foment dissension within the higher levels of the organization, what eventually led to the breakup of the League.

It must be said that MacInnes during his lifetime visited Japan and China countless times, even working in Peking to implement public transportation. From 1916 to 1927, he spent long periods in China developing business interests. He was the only foreign director of the Kwontong Tramway Company from 1919 to 1924. His Chinese venture came to a sudden end when the Chinese revolutionary government expropriated his company. For MacInnes it had been "seized by Bolsheviks and blackguards."

Not only did he have an experience-based knowledge of Asian culture, as he had studied Chinese culture, traditions and history extensively in Dr. Morrison's then famous private library in Peking, but also he had been taught Asian philosophies by Samuel Couling, then a famous scholar of the Orient.

MacInnes was thus considered an expert in Canada on Asian culture and when the Canadian Minister of Trade and Commerce, George Foster, decided to visit China in 1911, it was MacInnes who drafted the itinerary and briefed the official.

His experience in Asia led Minister of the Interior Frank Oliver to commission him to draw a new Immigration Policy in 1909. As a lawyer, in 1910, he drew up the Canadian Immigration Act, the Anti-Opium Act, and the Dominion Northwest Water Power Regulations. He had also been asked to make a report on Indian title to land in Canada. His report, *On the Indian Title*, is historically significant as it stated that British Columbia Natives were unfairly dispossessed from the lands they had occupied for millennia.

It is at this busy period of his life that Tom, already in his middle age, took the pen and started writing poetry, eventually joining the League of Western Writers. The first book of verse of this brilliant poet, *Romance of the Lost*, was published in 1908. His second, *In Amber Lands*, mostly a reprint of the first book, was issued a year later. And his third volume, a work of interesting originality, *The Rhymes of a Rounder*, whose title seemed inspired by Robert Service's 1912 *Rhymes of a Rolling Stone*, was published in 1913, with the spelling MacInnes replacing its former spelling.

After spending years in Peking, MacInnes returned to British Columbia in 1924. That decade marked a change in MacInnes' outlook on life. Until then, he had been deeply liberal in his attitude, appreciative of Vancouver's ethnic diversity, but also opposed to any Puritan restrictions. His ideal society was the one of early pioneers, the Wild West, where there were very few rules and law enforcement, but order was kept by the pioneers' inner sense of honor and dignity. Like he explained, drunkenness was rarely to be seen in that Golden Age; people knew how to behave and did not need to fear the wrath of God or the State to behave properly.

He was an Imperialist, in the same vein as Cecil Rhodes and the Liberal Imperialists of the 19th and early 20th century. The British Empire had a role in bringing Enlightenment to the rest of the globe. It had a mission to spread freedom around the globe. It was a pacifying mission that had to be pursued; it was in a certain way, "the white man's burden."

But in the 1920s, his perceptions started to change. The Orientals whom he deeply respected started becoming more populous in British Columbia. The discourse of the Asian Exclusion League was not that radical after all.

He started writing in various media outlets like the *Toronto Saturday Night*, *Toronto Star Weekly*, *Vancouver Daily Province*, *Vancouver Daily Sun* and *Canadian Western Lumberman*. One of the subjects that was covered in his articles was the "Yellow Peril," although he never himself used that expression. The man who had been an advocate of Chinese and Canadian friendship and mutual understanding was realizing that Canada as a white country was threatened. And the menace was very strong in British Columbia.

In 1927, he published his first and only political book, *The Oriental Occupation of British Columbia*, a collection of earlier articles on the Asian question. It must be said that at the time, the subject was openly discussed by politicians and there was no taboo like there is today on this issue. The Asian Exclusion League boasted 20,000 members and anti-Asian articles were common in the press. Actually, there was even a paper devoted to the question, *The Anti-Asiatic Weekly*. In this newspaper, the works of another Canadian poet, Hilda Glynn-Ward (Hilda G. Howard) were often published. She had herself authored a novel on the Asian question, *The Writing on the Wall*, in order to warn her fellow citizens of the menace mass Asian immigration represented in Canada.

Even if the tone of MacInnes' book is straightforward, it is no way the work of a "fanatic or unsubstantial alarmist." After all, he had always been fascinated by Asian culture and had always entertained harmonious and respectful relationships with the Orientals. Furthermore, he had enjoyed diversity since his boyhood and had fond memories of Blacks in his hometown of Dresden — the city having welcomed many former slaves — as well as of the Natives of Chinook, whom he had appreciated. He never "had any anti-Oriental phobia or Nordic nonsense about color such as afflicts some of our people." "Some of the best friends (he) ever had, who more than once proved themselves friends in time of great need at home and abroad when those of (his) own race would have let (him) sink without a trace, were Chinese and Japanese." Moreover, he preferred "some of their food, some of their fabrics, much of their culture, and more of their religion" to his own.

But this did not mean that this admiration was blind, and he knew "what they would do with us if they had the upper hand." According to MacInnes, it was a question of preserving the province's British character. He mentioned in the book joining a "non-partisan group of British Columbians (...) recently formed for the purpose of securing by legislative enactment some effective measure of relief," devoted to "save British Columbia, so far as lawfully and peacefully may be done, from the dangers now threatening its future by reason of Oriental occupation."

The group he was a representative of was the ABC Group[2], a group of businessmen, created in 1928 to defend themselves against Asian competition. At that time, even if "trade unions[3]

---

[2] WARD, Peter. *White Canada Forever*, Third Edition, Montreal, McGill-Queen's University Press, 2002, p. 135.
[3] Unions like the Workingmen's Protective Association and Knights of Labor openly opposed Oriental immigration.

became one the primary vehicles of anti-Oriental sentiment,"[4] the historian Peter Ward registered more than 100 nativist and anti-Oriental organizations in British Columbia, like the White Canada Association and the Asian Exclusion League. They had followed the path of the first Anti-Chinese Society born in 1873, which had started a long sequel of similar organizations, among which we would find the Anti-Chinese Association and the Canadian Anti-Chinese League of Locksley Lucas. But the anti-Oriental feeling was not only limited to civil societies. Politicians were often addressing the Oriental question openly. Even Premier John Oliver was among the opponents to Asian immigration, just like the Minister of Labour A. M. Manson, a prominent nativist, only surpassed by H. H. Stevens, the political torch bearer of Asian exclusion.

As mentioned above, MacInnes was far from sharing the usual prejudices held in those days by many British Columbians. He did not oppose their implementation because of their supposed uncleanliness or their presumed vicious ways in regard to opium and prostitution or lawlessness. His main argument was a demographic one, stressing that their "increase in the country would be disastrous to those already in occupation of it; especially if such intruding race be very prolific and very difficult to assimilate."

Like a West Coast senator had put it, "The main objection to the Chinese is that they are not of our race and cannot become a part of ourselves. We cannot build up a homogeneous people in Canada with races of that description, a population totally alien to ours."[5]

Already, in 1882, we could read in an editorial that "unless some immediate and urgent steps are taken to restrict this heathen invasion the rapid deterioration and ultimate extinction

---

[4] *Ibid.*, p. 48.
[5] *Ibid.*, p. 22.

of this Province as a home for the Anglo-Saxon race must ensue."[6]

Actually, in MacInnes' opinion, the problem was not the Asians per se, but multiracialism. As he wrote it, using the Belgian example, "racial differences mean weakening, both in peace and war, of the structure of any nation unfortunate enough to be pounded of such elements." Homogeneity is the key to a successful thriving nation. Multiculturalism is a plague for any nation. Thus, "the man who would put party advantage before the purity of his home is not worth calling a man. But to almost a great a degree, I think, a man should be concerned for the purity of his race; that is for keeping the blood stream of it free from any alien blood which will not improve it, or at least which may conflict with it in an ethnological or temperamental way, however excellent such alien blood may be in itself, and in its own kind. A mix of sugar and salt is the spoiling of both." It would then be mentally dishonest to assume that MacInnes held on to a hierarchy of races, but he was clearly a "separatist" or "ethnodifferentialist" to use a modern term. In his opinion, Canada had been, from its inception, a Nordic country mostly made up of Scots, English, and Nordic French from Normandy. Therefore, immigration had to come from the Nordic countries, to avoid altering its demographic balance. Thus, he also vehemently opposed accepting immigrants "of the Levant and the Near East who will never work with their hands on land in Canada," and also "Jews, Greeks (and) Armenians."

He also thought, like most union representatives of his time, that working conditions were being lowered due to mass Asian immigration. Today, if the Left has become a strong advocate for mass immigration from the Third World, it was not yet the case a century ago and the unions had been at the forefront of Asiatic exclusion, and had played a key role in the founding of the Asiatic Exclusion League.

---

[6] *Ibid.*, p. 32.

Those who supported Oriental immigration were capitalists who saw the cheap labor as a way to cut down the production costs. Two of the most prominent supporters of immigration had been Andrew Onderdonk, a capitalist contractor in the 1880s who had imported 1,500 Chinese workers for the railway to ensure inexpensive labor, and Robert Dunsmuir who had used Chinese scabs to smash a miner strike.

For MacInnes, "the short-sighted commercial greed of our own people, eager for quick profit, at any cost to the future generations of their own kin, is responsible for these Asiatic colonies having been planted and frequently reinforced during the past forty years."

Asians, both Chinese and Japanese, were willing to accept lower wages and harsher conditions, accepting this fate without complaining. This made the Asian potential workers very attractive to businessmen who saw them as cheap substitutes to local workers. Ironically, if whites who opposed Oriental immigration are today labeled "white supremacists" by historians, a more appropriate expression would be "white nationalists," as the real white supremacist attitudes were rather held by the exploiters who made them come here as near slaves. And it is these rich white supremacists who forced politicians, the "gangsters of both parties," to open the floodgates. They somehow thought that the Asians would remain in their submissive role forever.

The Asian frugality and resilience also served Chinese and Japanese entrepreneurs who could enjoy lesser benefits in order to gain larger market parts and eventually control the province's economy, just like they had done in Hawaii. With "their lower economic standard," they would manage to drive the white businessmen out. Asians also had another advantage: unlike whites whose business partnerships were based on their short-term monetary gains, Asians, being more ethnocentric, favored their own kind in business relationships.

Furthermore, he proved to be prophetic in forecasting the rise of China in the world market, warning that one day, "instead of our people manufacturing a surplus of goods and seeking a market for them in China, it will be the other way about."

In conclusion, based on those demographic and economic elements, he wrote "if there be no policy of Oriental Exclusion, rigidly enforced, then British Columbia and much of Alberta, before this century ends, will be largely occupied and controlled by Orientals."

"All we demand," MacInnes wrote, "is the dominance of our own race. We struggle to prevent our average white citizen from being displaced by Chinese and Japanese in the commercial, industrial and agricultural life of British Columbia."

His solutions were multifaceted. First, he wished to cut immigration drastically and end family reunification. With Orientals being one British Columbian out of 12, and having a birthrate "three times higher" than whites, he felt that immigration coupled with their "natural born increase" would allow them to eventually take over the land. Allowing their wives to come and establish families would foster their demographic boost, especially that when only adult males were taken into consideration, Asians represented one man out of five, according to a Bureau of Provincial Information report dated of 1927.

In 2016, minorities, almost all from Asian origins, were totaling 30% of British Columbia's population and in some cities, Chinese nationals were already a majority.

He also proposed to adopt some of the policies Asian countries applied. In fact, Japanese "would not tolerate an invasion of Japan, however peaceful it might seem" and, like the Chinese, had many restrictions imposed on foreigners to make them feel unwelcome. In Japan, products solely bought by whites were heavily taxed. In China, foreigners were limited to certain quarters and were required to remain there. Surely China and

Japan would not condemn policies they themselves applied at home!

MacInnes also proposed a remigration program based on voluntary departures, just like it had been practiced in South Africa with East Indian coolies. Restrictions would necessarily encourage them to leave and return to their motherland.

All these policies combined together would ensure British Columbia remained a white province "for more than a generation or two longer."

If the British Columbians were aware and conscious of the threat Asian immigration represented, he felt that Eastern Canadians did not care and were the reason why Ottawa refused to take action. However, he thought their support was crucial and wished Canadians coast to coast, nativists, Klansmen, French Canadians and all, to rally under the banner of "Keep Canada Canadian." That was a statement that did not draw unanimity in the 1920s. At that time, Canada was still a Dominion and there was no Canadian citizenship. If the Canadian government had power on certain issues, its inhabitants were still British subjects.

MacInnes was already considering himself a Canadian nationalist, emphasizing the need for a Canadian citizenship, and like his father before him, for a Canadian mint. He was not a chauvinistic nationalist, but he believed that every nation should hold the rein of its destiny. That is not to say that he opposed British imperialism. In fact, just like Joseph Conrad, he thought that it was a duty for the British to enlighten the other peoples of the Earth. For him, the Empire was the torchbearer of freedoms around the world: "If the British go down, then European civilization goes down, and more widely and disastrously than it did when the virtue of the Romans decayed. The British Empire breaks, then the British ideals of fair play, free speech, personal liberty and the right to be different will all be submerged in scattered systems of states, swinging uneasily from majority imposition of mass stupidity to dictatorships of some group of bakers or a self-selected oligarchy of Bolsheviks, or maybe to some eventual machine-built tyranny of businessmen over all, achieving the standardization of beehive, to be followed, in time, by revolts and anarchy."

In March 1932, Tom MacInnes decided to get actively involved in Canadian politics. He was among the co-founders of the Nationalist League of Canada, a mild political organization devoted to the defense of Canadians' rights, but that would later be involved in incidents with the Left.

The reason why the Nationalist League was later linked by some historians to Fascism is probably because about a year after its foundation, it merged with other political organizations, including some openly Fascist ones, to form a short-lived United Nationalists of Canada. The marriage did not last and soon the Nationalist League departed from this union to resume its independent activities.

Despite no source supporting this claim, it has been written by several historians who went even further that MacInnes had joined the Canadian Union of Fascists. Once again this assertion may come from a certain confusion: his Nationalist League was located in suite 406 of the Lumbermen's Building, a building that had also been used by the Canadian Guard and their gray shirts, a small Fascist formation issued from the short-lived Fascisti of Canada. But except for this coincidence, which is due to the fact that the owner of the Lumbermen's Building was sympathetic to the Right, and the fact that the League had united for some time with Fascists, nothing corroborates these claims of MacInnes being openly or secretly Fascist.

During this politically active period of his life, MacInnes put bread and butter on his table with radio talk shows, hosted on the Canadian Broadcasting Corporation (CBC). He was often criticized for his on-air appearances; some listeners labeling him a Fascist, although at that time the term was already used as a generic epithet against Rightists. He used his microphone to denounce the red menace as well as the "Yellow Peril." He was once sued, in 1937, by a unionist he had accused of importing "trouble" into British Columbia. MacInnes won the libel suit, which was the first libel suit brought against a radio talk show in the history of the province.

Interestingly, despite his opposition to Oriental immigration, he saw in a positive light the reawakening of Japan. Not only did he oppose a Japanese boycott in October 1938, but six years earlier, he had publicly defended the invasion of Manchuria.

Nevertheless, probably because of the many controversies surrounding him, the CBC canceled his program in November 1938. Although no sources were found on this very subject, it is likely that he continued on another radio station.

The controversies were far from over for MacInnes. In 1939, the Canadian Nationalist League was accused of having ties with the Canadian Nationalist Party, an accusation mostly unfounded as that Fascist party had ceased to exist the year before, after the merge with Adrien Arcand's own National Social Christian Party to form the National Unity Party of Canada.

During the Second World War, MacInnes drifted away from the spotlight, only reemerging to publish a last poetry book, *In the Old of My Age*, in 1947. At that time, he was living modestly, even asking the Western Writer Guild for financial help at the end of his life. The man who had been among the most celebrated poets of his days died almost forgotten on February 11, 1951.

Rémi Tremblay

INTRODUCTION TO MACINNES' POETRY

Although he has mostly been forgotten by now, Tom MacInnes was a Canadian poet of repute in his era and this even though he only started writing in his middle age. Interestingly, this unlikely poet wrote nothing until he was over thirty and little before he was forty, but by fifty-one had written the bulk of his work. Despite such a short writing career, he left a great variety of poems, covering different styles and themes.

Although E. K. Brown wrote in his *On Canadian Poetry* that he was "never so broadly popular as (William) Drummond or (Robert) Service," probably the most famous Canadians poets of the beginning of the 20th century, MacInnes' contemporary critics were generally enthused by his verses. For example, in *The Toronto Globe* of September 23, 1923, we could read that he was "a poet of considerable power and daring." *The Canadian Police Gazette*, December 1926, went further by stating that "Canada has two poets who have dared to be original: and that is the only thing Canadians do not dare, as a rule. These two are Tom MacInnes and Wilson MacDonald."

V. B. Rhodenizer, in *Handbook of Canadian Literature*, published in 1930, explained that "his artistic worth has been underestimated, especially by those who cannot dissociate their aesthetic judgments from their opinions as to the soundness or unsoundness of the ideas embodied in a work of art. In both fantastic romance and Epicurean philosophy MacInnes holds a unique position in Canadian poetry." Author William Arthur Deacon shared this opinion, describing MacInnes as "the great unknown of Canadian poetry, though one of the few whose work is likely to be read by future generations."

In a 1933 talk on Canadian poets of the early 20th century, Charles G. D. Roberts, considered the "Father of Canadian Poetry," said: "Preeminent among these is Tom MacInnes, standing somewhat apart from the stream of our poetry, and tracing the inheritance of his very individual talent to François Villon and Edgar Allan Poe, with an occasional dash of Keats."

It would be extremely hard to give a definite judgment on MacInnes' style or to confine him in a specific literary movement, as he loved to play with the forms, adopting different approaches towards poetry during his short but fruitful career. Once again, even if they were generally positive as noted above, 20th-century critics had difficulty categorizing him and what they highlighted from his prose varied greatly from one another.

Thus, in 1917, Deacon wrote of "the distinctive note of his poetry is in its dissolute cadence, its drunken rhymes, and a certain reckless goodwill. His metres often have a happy-go-lucky felicity which can be the result of nothing but inebriation of soul." Stephens agreed and highlighted his "light, easy verse that dismissed smugness and respectability with unconcerned humour ... an amused detachment underlies his work, as though poetry were merely one form of expression, as good as any other." He believed "that joy and delight, rather than the prevalent melancholic outpourings of the soul, were essential to poetry." However, John M. Elson, an academic from Toronto University, would by contrast talk of his "laconic stanzas, with their surprise blending of the homely and the bizarre," while J. Arthur P. Caley described the "remote and medieval atmosphere of blended Nordic and Moorish beauty" in his poems.

How could opinions differ so much and present the author in such different lights?

Basically because if there are subjects or forms that were thoroughly exploited by MacInnes' pen, he remained faithful to his youthful dreams of adventure, exploring all kinds of avenues as the reader of this anthology will notice.

The first observation a modern reader will make is the diversity of unfamiliar forms employed by MacInnes. Villanelles, cantels, mirelles and ballads virtually obsessed MacInnes who took "easily to difficult French forms of centuries ago, using them for contemporary and commonplace themes" to quote J. Arthur P. Caley.

Forms became a quest on their own, a passion for MacInnes who delved into the past to bring back to life forms disappeared long ago. Medieval France became his prime investigative field, although he only read through translations, not mastering any foreign language, a handicap that did compel him to state that "every Canadian should know French". In fact, he went as far as declaring that "The French (were) civilized beyond other races."

The villanelle, probably unfamiliar to most 21st-century readers, was inspired by the songs the French serfs of the Middle Ages, the "tillers of the soil," or villains as they were called. It is derived from the songs they used to sing the fields. In MacInnes' opinion, those men, who would eventually become peasants in France and the yeomanry in England, "had more freedom than may be enjoyed by millions where totalitarian state control is established."

The villanelle was originally a "loose roundelay with double refrain," but became known as poem of 19 lines, with a return to starting point at the end. In French, it counts only two rhymes, but in Canada it is written with a runaround of rhymes. The length is fixed with six stanzas of three verses, except the last that counts four. As most specialists agree, *Villanelle of Mutton* and *Tiger of Desire* are MacInnes' most successful and typical poems of this sort.

The mirelle, that MacInnes invented in Quebec, is another form inspired from France. Interestingly no other poet used this five stanza form. The mirelle is made up of five five-lined stanzas, the first stanza rhyming *abaab*, the second *bcbbc*, and so on, until in the final stanza the *a* rhyme recurs in the second and last lines. *Mirelle of Found Money* and *Mirelle of the Good Bed*, despite their unlikely subjects, are perfect examples of this unique style.

Another form invented by MacInnes is the cantel, a three four-lined stanza poem, the first and last rhyming *aaba*, and the second *bbab*. Despite brevity, MacInnes explained, it allowed to "give utterance."

E. K. Brown rightly noted that "in general MacInnes uses the mirelle for the same kind of theme and tone as the ballade, and the cantel for the same kind of theme and tone as the villanelle."

Tom MacInnes was particularly proud of his poetic inventions and humorously boasted: "So far I have written the best cantels to be found in English. Same I would say for mirelles." Being the only poet using those forms, his assertions were unchallenged!

MacInnes also explored epics in an original way, although critics have often said that he had been less successful in this venture than in other forms, an opinion we may disagree with reading *Fey* or *Lonesome Bar*.

He also touched upon more common forms like the sonnets — whose best were according to him *October* and *Content* — and the ballads. "The ballad, as a combination of song and dance, was universal long before Latin was contrived. Probably it was familiar to folk of the Stone Age," he explained. With the ballad, he could come back to the melodies of early poetry and found the Scottish ballads the best in this regard. *The Ballade of Action* and *The Ballade of the Free Lance* capture the original spirit of the style.

That last point concerning the music of words and forms was crucial for MacInnes. If form and its exploration fascinated him, he still thought that music was the most important element of poetry; "if it seems musical it is musical. If it seems a sound it is a sound." He felt there was no rule for music, only feeling really mattered. That is why he personally preferred ballads and villanelles. But still, he continued to touch upon different forms as his "ear demanded variations."

Despite being obsessed by the form of poetry, he refused the notion of syllabic measures, something he denounced as "pedant." According to him, measures "make dry bones of poetry." One must follow his ear and the "flow of his pleasure." That vision of poetry does not really differ from Ezra Pound's as expressed in *ABC of Reading*.

The dominance of feeling over rules led him to sometimes overlook English grammar. "When I am called upon to choose between a rule of grammar and my ear," he explained, "always I bow to my ear." Elson qualified him of "futurist" for that tendency to disregard grammar.

MacInnes was famous for his many puns, although some may not be as accessible to modern readers as they used to be for his contemporaries.

As for the actual content of these poems, he explored themes frequently used by poets from all ages, from love to death. One though cannot fail to see that one of his recurring subjects is the change of mindset that occurred in his life. "It would seem that after years of colorful and intense life he remains a boy seeking his own amusement; complaining loudly enough when he is hurt in the pursuit of it; then straightway forgetting at the prospect of any new pleasure," a *Toronto Globe* critic noted on November 24, 1923.

Another theme often touched upon was religion, especially in the long didactic poem *High Low Along*. He appreciated religion's appeal to make people seek personal improvement, but despised the sectarian or Puritan version of it, with its emphasis on developing a sense of guilt. He also saw many contradictions in religions, both Christianity and Buddhism. Of this latter topic, it must be said that he understood Eastern philosophy from Zen to Lao-tzu, and some of his poems prove it beyond any doubt. The poet of the Canadian Far West had never totally left the fascinating Far East.

Although raised Christian, he believed that conscience was the barometer to behave properly and that everyone was able to set for himself a code of conduct, based on the knowledge gained with his own experience. In this sense, he was a liberal, although as the pioneers were, with very limited rules imposed upon them and believing in unlimited freedom, although not the abusing of it. "Nothing is wrong if I do not hurt" was his personal motto.

Interestingly, he cannot be considered a Rationalist either as he found the tenants of science as sectarian as the Puritans themselves. If in his opinion, a human was simply an animal that managed to gain supremacy because of his "co-operating hands," he remained doubtful of science... just as he was doubtful of God.

Overall, one can see in MacInnes a Romantic, in the literary sense of it, but one cannot agree with Elson who qualified him as "a philosophizing pleasure-seeker, frequently in difficulty." MacInnes was much more complex than a simple Epicurean.

Rémi Tremblay

ANTHOLOGY

Rubric

Let thro' a villanelle be sent,
   Rhythmic as arithmetic,
My senescent sentiment!

Simple so may be the trick
   Enriching mediocrity—
Simple as a limerick.

Sometimes brooding moodily
   Over what made things begin,
Thins convincement comes to me:

It's worth the world if we may win
   For ourselves deliverance
Unto beyond of origin!

Words of mine have slim chance
   Of clarifying what is meant
By such a cryptic utterance.

But this maun do the rubric
   To the verses subsequent—
Rhythmic as arithmetic
   For senescent sentiment!

In the Old of My Age

A. ADVENTURE/ACTION

Amber Lands

1

In a luminous valley once I awoke
 To the amber sound of lutes;
And I ate of the bread of a sylvan folk,
With elvish herbs and savory roots,
 And I drank of the innocent wines
Made by their maidens from mandarin fruits
Pluckt from low-lying luxurious vines
 In the somnolent heart of the valley.

And the sylvan folk have a simple creed:
To make with their hands whatever they need,
 And to live and be kind in the Sun:
To be one with the good brown Earth, and eat
Good things the Sun hath shone upon
 Till they be ripe and sweet:
And watch the flocks meanwhile that feed
 In the blue up-lands of the valley.

And aptly enough they sow and spin
In manner of antique industry,
And metals they mould and various glass
 And motley pottery,
Taught by priests of a gentle class
 In league with pale high Powers,
For whom they have builded singular towers
 In a grove of cypress trees,—
Towers of granite and bronze, wherein
Magic they make and medicine,
Or busied with their dim auguries
The hollows of space and cycles immense
They measure with intricate instruments.

But I mind how more it pleasur'd me
In the drowsy grass for hours and hours

To lie with the faintly conscious flowers,
  Far up on the slope of the valley;
Or run with the younger sylvan folk,
  So handsome and sturdy they be,
At play in a forest of maple and oak,
  A-romping healthily—
A-romping unkempt and all at their ease,
And kindly under the kindly trees
Doing whatever and ever they please
Consistent with courtesy.

O in youth I sail'd unusual seas,
And still I recall me lands like these,
Where they do whatever they please, dear Lord,
  Whatever and ever they please!

2

Roaming I met the gentle maid
Whom forest-folk and hunters call
The Chatelaine of Ronzival.
'Twas under a cliff in the everglade
Where the icy waters bubble forth;
In velvet green was she array'd
After the fashion of the North:
O gentle maid, for thy heart's ease
Venture with me far over the seas!

There is a room in Ronzival
Rich with bronze, and panell'd all
  In oak grown dull with time:
About the lancet windows there
  Masses of ivy climb:
And some few roses, fair, O fair,
Wave in the Northern summer air!

The Sun was sinking thro' the pines,
While I was guest of the Chatelaine;

Ruddily in slanting lines
Thro' each lancet window-pane
It lit the panell'd inner wall
Of that room in Ronzival,
With its bronze and quaint designs
And stilted things armorial:
O gentle maid, for thy heart's ease,
Venture with me far over the seas!

At table by a window-seat
The gentle maid sat long with me,
And shyly of her courtesy
   She bade me drink and eat;
Out of a hammer'd silver dish
She chose me cakes and comfits fine,
From a flagon twisted dragonish
   She pour'd me amber wine.
O gentle maid, our game is play'd,
The dragon is calling, calling!—
While over the cliffs in the everglade
   The lonely waters falling
Blanch at the sound, and shiver afraid,—
   Aye, 'tis the dragon calling!

With chilling breath and bitter rime
Cometh soon the winter-time:
Ah, see how she hath grown so frail,
Her form so slight, her face so pale!
I fear the gnomes of Niffelheim
   Will take her craftily,
And in a vault with marble stay'd,
Where long-forgotten saints have pray'd,
Her delicate body will be laid,
   Cover'd with greenery:
While down the ragged silver steep
Where the gnomish waters creep
Somnolent, sonorous, deep,

With her ancient friends
Lost to thee her soul shall sleep
   Till the legend ends!
Nay, gentle maid, for thy heart's ease,
Venture with me far over the seas,
And we shall go free of their wizard hands,
Away and away in the amber lands!

3

From Mozambique I sought Zambar
   On board an old felucca:
And nigh the Mosque in the Moon Bazar
   I got me a chanted hookah:
Its outer bowl was all inscribed
With golden arabesqueries,
And cryptic formules founded on
The amorous songs of Solomon,
   Or Paynim mysteries.
But the learned Moulah whom I bribed
   Gave me no meaning of these:
Only, observing the courtesies,
To me he show'd, while the fire in it glow'd,
   A manner of taking my ease;
From the worry of life, with its folly and strife,
   A marvellous good surcease.
And the years have come, and the years have flown,
   But the hookah still hath power;
And many a scintillating hour
I win in the midst of miseries,
Smoking aright in the manner unknown,
   With suitable ceremonies.

And haply, if someone understands,
   And shares the hour with me,
As once I mind at Joloban,
Tala Tavern, Joloban,
Where I met the scholar man,

With his sister Zulie,
As then, if someone understands,
  And shares the hour with me,
We talk of ships and caravans,
  And all the valorous merchantry
Of purple seas and yellow sands
  Beyond Crim-Tartary.

4

I have my chanted hookah still,
But now, when its fragrant bowl I fill,
And its dreamful smoke I draw and blow,
Watching it go—slow—so—
Round and round the carbuncle glow—
O then I remember things like these,
How in youth I sail'd unusual seas,
  And I would a-roving go.
I have my chanted hookah still,
But the core of the world has not been seen,
And lands unknown yet lie between
  The roots of Ygdrasil.
And what of that garden Hesperides,
  Forgotten this long, long while?
And the palmy cliffs of Hy-Brasil
  And good Saint Brendan's Isle?
And they tell in Arabian histories
Of venturings to ravish me,
And delectable zones of heathenry
  Down under the Lost Indies!
But now I would know of their verity,
  And to what each tale alludes,
So I will again to the solitudes,
  And the winds I will be loving,
And leave these weary latitudes
  And for the love of God go roving:
While yet the soul of me understands
  The ways that lead to amber lands—

A vagabond here if you please, among these,
   With my unheeded song,
But a rover by right thro' amber lands—
Thro' the amber light of amber lands
   That I have loved so long—so long!

Lonesome Bar

ADVENTURE/ACTION

Laughter

Glory be, the corner is turned,
   And we've given the slip to the old Hoodoo!
Come, Moriarty, I think we've earned
   The right to loaf, don't you?
Our score is paid, and we've money galore,
Enough to last us a month or more,
   And never a thing to do!
You're hungry you say? Well, I am too,
But stroll this way for half a mile,
Sure the sun is good this afternoon,
Good for a pasty-faced gossoon!
   Like you, d'ye hear, Moriarty?
Aye, 'tis a blessed afternoon
For you, ye prison-faced gossoon!
And you're lucky that some are dead!
I'm talking too loud? Aw—go on!
That red liquor has gone to my head,
   But I know what I'm doing I tell you!
There's none in this town that you're frightened to meet
   And I'm not the sort that would sell you.
But you're hungry you say—you want to eat?
Well, come with me to Easy Street,
And I'll show you a tavern to your taste—
   To your taste, d'ye hear, Moriarty?

*   *   *   *   *   *

Aw, take your time, boy! What's the haste?
There, where you see that ugly baste
   Ayont the Barbecue,
Where the lettering is half erased,
   'Twas gold when it was new.
Make out that name there if you can
With your cock-eye: *The Black-and-Tan*:
That's it: 'tis kept by a Mexican,
   And that's where we dine, Moriarty!

It has a long, deep-raftered room
In the Mission style; 'tis a man's room.
And sure you'll like this Mexican,
A fellow to follow a light amour,
A picaroon and a troubadour,
   Much of your sort, Moriarty!

* * * * * *

Hey, Miguel! Come hear me tell
   This hungry friend of mine
How this joint of yours is for epicures
Who like a shady place to dine!
See this long, deep-raftered room,
Half alight and half in gloom,
And yonder a cactus red in bloom,
   Just to your taste, Moriarty!
Somehow it puts me in mind of Yvette:
You remember—little Yvette?
Will you ever forget that night when she trackt us
Into the old Savoy, and cried
For us to take her East again,
And we hadn't the price—and then—and then—
All right, Miguel, by the window here:
That horrible rope—it turns me queer
To think of it yet—poor little Yvette—
   She always was fond of a cactus!
   Yes, beer, Moriarty, beer!
Then order whatever you wish—a dish
Of chowder, perhaps a sole,
Or some foreign thing en casserole,
They're great on that line here!
You leave it to me? Well, on the whole
Of things come far and things come near
I fancy an onion omelette
   With bacon on the side!
Or what do you say to a steak Creole
   With sweet potatoes fried?

ADVENTURE/ACTION

  You like these things done Spanish,
    And it isn't a Friday yet?
New raisins then and a pint of port
To finish on; they say 'tis good
To iron the blood of a broken sport,
    And they keep it here in the wood.

* * * * * *

Moriarty, what are ye thinking of?
Be easy, lad! By the lovely dove,
Myself—I could sit in this place for hours!
Those red flowers in the window set
Where the wind gets at them—damn it all
To me they seem to lift and fall
Like the red skirts of little Yvette,
    When she danced at the carnival!
Moriarty, lad, if we only knew—
Eh? O, yes! That's all—thank you—
That's all, Miguel, thank you—thank you—
    But serve it up hot and Spanish!
And now while I roll me a cigarette
  Tune up that old guitar
    And sing while we wait, Moriarty!
Sing new songs, and sing till you banish
Out of my heart this grey regret;
    Sure that's what you're for, Moriarty!
Sing new songs to that old guitar
Of things come near and things come far,
While I forget, forget, forget,
Watching the rings from my cigarette
Rise to the rafters and vanish!

* * * * * *

Watching the rings! How each of them alters!
Each of them alters and alters—and alters—
Moriarty!—see—they're swinging like halters
    Just over our heads as they climb!

And after—and after—and after—
Christ! hear that devilish laughter—
That devilish gurgle and laughter!
And there!—see there how each rafter
Is red—dripping red all the time!

* * * * * *

No, no, Miguel—I'm well, man—I'm well!
My nerves, that's all! It's passing—this spell:
Moriarty can tell—there's nothing to tell!
Roll me another cigarette,
   And sing, damn you! Sing and forget
   That laughter—ghost laughter—hereafter!

Lonesome Bar

ADVENTURE/ACTION

Ballade of the Free Lance

Let me face some bright hazard
   Against this rowdy World for you!
A foe to strike, a friend to guard,
   Or the looting of some rascal crew,
   O, the like of this I'm taking to
As on my way I make advance,
   And queer vicissitudes come through,
Full of adventure and multiple chance!

So far, you see, I've not been slain:
   Tho' now and then I've sought to raid
Some richly opportune domain,
   Only to find the plan I made
   Baffled by engine or ambuscade:
But I salute the circumstance,
   And slip aside; O the World is laid
Full of adventure and multiple chance!

And while I'm free to ride ahead,
   With here or there some prize in view,
Few dangers of the way I dread,
   Tho' oft my hungriness I rue:
   Still, betimes a crust will do
Cracking fine to nonchalance,
   And every day the World is new,
Full of adventure and multiple chance!

For me the road of many directions—
   For me the rhyme of long romance!
For me the World of imperfections—
   Full of adventure and multiple chance!

Rhymes of a Rounder

Ballade of Action

No fat security hath charms
   To keep me always satisfied:
What ho! Excursions and alarms!
   A scheme, a plot, a ripping tide
   Of rude events to prick my pride,
Or crack the shell of my conceit
   Upon the edge of things untried!
This is the fate that I would meet.

Now let some bully thing intrude,
   And bugle to the soul of me!
I grow stale with quietude,
   And this too safe monotony:
   O good my friend or enemy
Call me back to the battling street!
   For high low variety—
This is the fate that I would meet.

To more than keep oneself alive
   Is the way to live when all is said:
To sight a prize, and chase and strive
   With strong will and cunning head
   For something surely more than bread,
Or from the bitter steal the sweet,
   And steal it while the risk is red—
This is the fate that I would meet.

To conquer finely, or to sink
   Debonair against defeat,
This is the rarest grace I think—
   This is the fate that I would meet.

Rhymes of a Rounder

ADVENTURE/ACTION

Lady of Ventures
Mirelle

Lady of Ventures weaving gold
   From next to nothing tell me, pray,
Some novel thing to do! Unfold
Some fine employ or project bold
   Or sly detour along my way!

From London town to far Cathay
   The many live in drab durance:
But evermore your colors play,
Lady of Ventures, grave or gay,
   Over the regions of Romance.

And some who find you sideways glance,
   Nor scorn to reach thro' gates obscure
Forbidden vistas that entrance,
And glimmer with caprice and chance
   To alter destinies grown dour.

Whether to some moonlit amour,
   Or quest of hidden treasury,
Or valiant or outlandish lure,
They follow you, and think for sure
   'Tis worth whatever the cost may be.

Thro' drear lanes of poverty,
   Thro' little shops, and garrets old,
I've seen you wander truantly,
And pass tiptoe, and beckon me—
   O Lady of Ventures weaving gold!

Rhymes of a Rounder

B. BRITISH EPICS AND NARRATIVES

For the Crowning of the King
An Ode

1

Ye sovran Stars! that in the deep
Of endless Night your courses keep,
    'Twas said of old
    That ye do hold
A mystic rein o'er human destinies!
That from the vast, exultant sweep
    Of your Eonian harmonies,
    Fateful thro' ethereal seas
      Enrythym'd cycles flow,
    Whose subtle volume sways
    The tide of nether days
      Forever 'tween the goals of weal and woe!
I am not vers'd in Magian mysteries,
    Nor dim, Chaldean lore—
Arcturus and the pallid Pleiades
I see as any peasant sees,
    Jewelling Heaven's floor—
Yet on the coronation morn
    Of him who is our ruler now,
    With simple heart would I implore
      That only sweetest influences
    From out the skies be borne![1]
O may no orb of red disaster fling
Malefic rays to mar a monarch's brow!
Shine out! Shine out, ye Stars of joy, and bring
A benison of peace upon the crowning of our King!

2

    Rise golden for the glorious day,
      O golden Sun!
    Blow, ye Winds! and waft away

---

[1] "Canst thou bind the sweet influences of Pleiades?"—Job.

    What clouds in envious array
Would frown upon a reign so well begun!
       O shining One!
   This day thy rounded skies shall ring
   With sound of Britons gathering,—
   And every Zone shall hear them sing
      God save the King!

3

No despot on a guarded throne
   Will Britons own!
No crafty council of the chosen few,
Such as the old Republics knew,
   Such as made proud Venice groan,
     Shall e'er undo
     Our long-descended liberty!
No oligarchy, rich with spoil
Of others' wealth and others' toil,
   Nor yet the whim of mere majority,
   That substitution for old tyranny,
     However it be term'd,
     Shall wrest from us what Magna Charta gave,
     And our first Edward's hand and seal confirm'd!
Behold! Around the World the royal standards wave!
   And yet in all our scatter'd States
     The humblest Briton—nay,
   The lowliest stranger that's within our Gates,
      In open day
   May say the thing that he would say,
And work and worship without let in his own chosen way!

4

    Outcast,
Forgotten tribes, in ages past,
  As by some direful tempest tossed,
Were scatter'd wide, and long 'mid alien nations lost,
   By plagues cut off, by foes harassed,

Yet thro' all change of time and place,
   While kingdoms rose, and kingdoms fell,
   And mighty empires moulder'd to decay,
In all those tribes a saving trace
   Of pride and faith invincible
Bespoke the instinct of a chosen race.
         At last
      There came a day
As if a dim-remember'd Voice were calling them away.
      Then in the weakest exile's breast
         'Gan burn a fever of unrest,—
   March on! March on! went up the cry
   As every morn they struck their tents
To journey with the Sun and seek the West,—
      They knew not why;
   But thus did their wandering recommence,
   Inspir'd by one o'ershadowing Influence!
      From tracts where still the savage Tartar roves,
      Beyond where Caspian's bitter waters spread,
      From regions of the old Egyptian dead,
         Or thro' Iberian orange-groves;—
         On Northern seas, or lost among
         Germanic forests' dark defiles,
         Of varied creed and divers tongue,
      All unwitting, tribe by tribe were led
Thro' legendary years to their predestin'd Isles.
         Let History tell
         What things thereafter in those Isles befell!
            Isolate by wrathful seas,
         How clan and tribe together fought
         With eager rage thro' iron centuries!
            How still they wrought
         Their rugged characters to a rough ideal
         Of equity and courage! How from it all
            Some inkling of their destiny,
            And their essential unity,
         Did weld them into loyal peace at last!
         How slowly as the years went past,

      And still with vague intent,
The corner-stone of empire square was laid
By scholar's pen, by warrior's blade,
      By wisdom of free Parliament,—
By noble deed of every class,
With steadfastness of that God-fearing mass
    Whose name no records now recall,—
        Freemen all!
Whether they dwelt in ploughman's hut or grey baronial hall.
   Then, fired once more with the will to roam,
   The younger sons forsook their Island home;
     They set their sails for every breeze,
   Their gallant vessels cut the foam
     Of unfamiliar seas,
   Till every port their daring ensigns knew,
And traffic'd or fought on every coast some roving British crew.
      No need to tell
      How now they dwell
      In every zone invincible!
   How 'tis their boast around the World,
   Where'er their banners are unfurled,
Essential as the very breath they draw,
   To 'stablish fast from age to age
   The Briton's glorious heritage,
The deep instinct of Liberty—the vigor of the Law!

5

    Way for the King!
Down Westminster's glorious aisle
With blare of trumpets, roll of drums,
   And sound of organs thundering,
On the royal pageant comes
In stately ancient order, while
All the pride of three old Kingdoms
    Follows after—wondering!

      O splendid Hour!
See knights and dames of cherished Chivalry,
With ermine deckt, with plumes atoss,
   And coronets ablaze,
And every quaint device that Heraldry
Can broider or emboss,
   To bring again a dream of Gothic days,
In right of old assurance standing forth!
   But, eloquent of vaster power,
   See notable 'mid these,
   The chieftains of the Empire over Seas!
Here from the white Dominion of the North,
And there from late-embattl'd Africa!
Here the gallants of the Southern Cross,
With those that rule in jewell'd India!
See them thronging, hushed and dense,
Between the storied walls from whence
  The marble images of men look down
Who wrought the Empire's eminence!
Hail to thee, Edward! Kneel for the crown
Worn by the Mother-Queen, whose pure renown
Won every nation's reverence!
Hail to thee, Edward! Mount the throne!
  That venerable chair
  Whose carven oak, so legends old declare,
  Enshrines the very stone
  That pillow'd Jacob's head, when far alone
  On Bethel plain his dreaming eyes
  Beheld a shining ladder rise
  In glorious portent to the skies.
Treasur'd long thro' patriarchal days,
  As pledge of grandeur yet in store,
That stone was borne by devious ways
  At last to Erin's shore;
And thus safe-kept thro' all its wanderings,
Lo! Ireland's, Scotland's, England's kings,

And kings that be all three,
Thereon in long ascendant line shew forth that dream and
    prophecy!

6

Keen be thy sword, O King!
Sternly thy peace maintain!
That he who sails the wave, and he who tills the soil,
And all who win their bread by honest toil,
May fear no foeman's ravening
Thro' all thy wide domain!
Far off from us be that most fatal hour
When guardian hands grow lax from long unchallenged
    power!
For man hath still a wolfish mind,
    Ensway'd of greed and lust;
And still o'er all the Earth we find
    No nation weaponless may trust
The justice of mankind.
    Keen be thy sword, O King!
Then Faith, secure from bigot's rage, shall flower
    In every form that listeth her, and Art,
    O'er seven seas awakening,
From her ethereal treasury shall dower
Thy throne with gifts of new and golden fashioning!
    Untrammel'd Science, on her endless quest,
        Shall march beneath thy standard's shadowing,
    Shall add to life unwonted zest,
    And wizard powers now all unguessed
        To man impart!
            O King!
Whate'er we did in days of yore,
Our greatest work lies yet before!
Be thine to keep the Empire's heart
        Sound at the core!

7

So shall we sing
God save the King!
  God guard his realms wide!
For him be happy years in store
  With that sweet Consort by his side,
Whose beauty Time hath lingered o'er—
  But courteous left untried!
O'ershadow them in all their ways,
And still, O God, if parlous days
  Should come beyond the ken
Of King and Prince and Councillors,
And all the Empire's Senators,
  As in time past be Thou again
Our trusted Guide!
And on us all be blessings multiplied
  E'en as thou wilt! Amen!

For the Crowning of the King

On Beacon Hill

1

Prone on a grassy knoll where runs the sea
In from the North Pacific, deep and blue,
Whose tide-ript waters many a century
But parted for the painted war-canoe,
Till Juan de Fuca and his swarthy crew
Sail'd on a treasure cruise to regions cold,
Idle I dream'd a summer evening through,
Watching the ruddy Western Sun enfold
The snowy-peaked Olympians in transient gold.

2

Our air hath yet some tang of Spanish days,
Some glow of stories fading from the past
Of pioneers, and wreckt and curious strays
From distant lands along this coast up-cast,
Since brave Vancouver, from his eager mast,
Beheld the island of his lasting fame,
And, veering to its pleasant shore, made fast
To raise our flag in George's royal name,
While group'd around his brawny tars gave loud acclaim.

3

Across the rocky harbor-mouth still fall
Echoes to tell of England's easy crown,
And timely bugles from the barracks call
A challenge to the careless little town
That lies like a pretty maid in tatter'd gown
'Mid tangled gardens, tempting one to halt
Where gnarled oaks, with ivy overgrown,
Are all accord with her one charming fault—
So drowsy nigh the hidden guns of Esquimalt.

4

And nonchalant lay I that afternoon,
The air a scent of wild white-clover bore,
And I could hear the tumult and the tune
Of tumbling waves along the pebbled shore;
Such gipsy joys to me were ever more
Than chase of gold or fame; but yet withal
I felt the first fine tremor o'er and o'er
Of some vast traffic without interval
To traverse soon these waterways imperial.

5

Where now some tug-boat leaves a smoky trail
To pencil on the air a coiling blot
Athwart the lighthouse, or the infrequent sail
Of some slow lumber-bark, or vagrant yacht,—
Where glides some British cruiser, grimly wrought,
Beside the schooners from the Bering seas,—
To largely feed the crowded world methought
Here soon shall pass great annual argosies
Full-freighted with the yield of prairie granaries.

6

And musing thus upon that gentle mound,
Far down the reach of waters to the right
I saw an Empress liner inward bound,
Speeding thro' the Narrows, trim and white,
And every moment growing on my sight,
Like something clear unfolding in a dream;
Her very motion was a clean delight,
That woke the sapphire sea to curl and cream
Smoothly off her curving prow and snowy beam.

7

And easily as up the Straits she roll'd,
My fancy rambled over her to see,

Bulging richly 'gainst her steely hold,
Bales of flossy silk stow'd solidly
With matted rice and tons of fragrant tea;
Or else, her quainter cargo fain to scan,
Wee China toys in silver filigree,
And cunning ivories of old Japan,
Pack'd with iris-woven rugs from Ispahan.

8

All hail to her! the white forerunner sent
From out the lavish West to rouse the old
Lethargic portals of the Orient,
Till all its stolid habitants be told
Of quick new modes of life, and manifold
Swift engines of exchange, and how by these
To run their times within a finer mould,
And from the rut of Chinese centuries
To reach for wider joys and soother luxuries.

9

O sure it is no small thing to be said
That under us the East and West have met!
And our red route shall yet be perfected
Around the World, and our old flag shall yet
Much vantage o'er its younger rivals get,
Whether it wave from Windsor's kingly pile,
Or on the farthest verge of Empire set,
 'Bove fearless towns, whose heart-strings all the while
Shall thrill to every chord from their old Mother-isle.

10

We feel the centre now, where'er we stand,
And touch community in everything,
Since Science, with her patient, subtle hand,
Hath snar'd the Globe as in a witch's ring,
And set all elements a-quivering
To our desire. What marvels more she'll show—

What new delights from Nature conjuring—
Small wit have I to guess, but this I know,
That more and more the scattered World as one must grow.

11

Then closer blend for empire—that is power:
No thing of worth e'er came of feebleness,
And union is the genius of the hour.
The virtues that by master-craft and stress
Wrought hugely on primeval palaces,
And 'stonish'd Egypt and great Babylon
With monuments of admirable excess,
Seem once again from out Oblivion drawn
To lighten o'er the Earth in unexampl'd dawn.

12

We front the threshold of a giant age,
Foremost still, but others follow fast;
We may not trust o'ermuch the written page,
Or measure with the measures of the past.
For all our millions, and our regions vast,
And arm'd array, in boastful numbers told,
To keep the treasures that our sires amass'd,
Hath need of statesmen lion-like to hold,
And still forestall the changing times alert and bold.

13

The impulse of a thousand centuries
Strikes upward now in our united race.
Not for a Roman triumph, but to ease
The intercourse of nations and to place
The social fabric on a happier base;
The very enginry of war abhorr'd,
So soon as may, is bended to erase
The stain and bloody ravage of the sword;
The vanquish'd now are all to equal right restor'd.

14

But cry contempt upon that sickly creed
That would not fire a shot to save its own,
Whose piety perverse doth only feed
The hope of leaner nations, bolder grown,
To tread the path that we have hewn alone:
'Twas not for them we found that path so hard—
'Twas not for them the Earth so thick was sown
With British dead! Nay, rather let us guard
The barest rock that flies our flag at all hazard.

15

And e'en for the sake of rich and plenteous peace,
Let mastery in arms be honor'd still!
So only shall the fear of foemen cease.
For this is naked truth, say what they will,
That when a people lose the power to kill
They count for naught among the sons of men;
Nor tongue, nor pen, nor art, nor workmen's skill
Can save their homes from alien ravish then,
Or lift their fallen capitols to place again.

16

Then give us rifles—rifles everywhere—
Ready rifles, tipt with bayonets!
And men of iron to lead, who little care
For parlor tactics or for social sets;
Red captains worthy of their epaulets;
Not rich men's sons to make a passing show,
Lace-loving fops or wooden martinets,
But clear-eyed stalwarts o'er the ranks, who know
How best to train a naval gun or trap a foe.

17

And tho' the burden and the fret of life
Still wear upon us with unequal weight,

We'll ne'er give way to fratricidal strife.
We are a people strong to tolerate,
Till form'd opinion tranquilly abate
Entrenched abuses of an earlier age,
Rather than, impatient, emulate
Those hapless nations that in sudden rage
Of revolution wreck their ancient heritage.

18

Our Saxon temper, that 'gainst Church and Crown,
And tyrant Castles of the feudal plan,
Made steady way until it wore them down,
And widen'd all their maxims till they ran
Current for the right of every man
Freely to change his state and circumstance,
Is virile yet unbrokenly to span
What gulf ahead, what unforeseen mischance,
Would threat the front of our magnificent advance.

19

And we have those whose dreams of betterment
Outrun their fleeting day; whose hearts' ideal
Beat evermore against discouragement,
In high endeavor not to cease till all
The bars to opportunity shall fall
Within the Union of the British bred;
Nor rest content until the mutual
Machinery of State be perfected,
So that no least of all our brethren go unfed.

20

I never saw Britannia carved in stone,
Or figured out in bronze, but loyally
I've thought what merit shall be all her own
In that great Brotherhood that's yet to be—
The crystal Empire of Futurity—
Whose equal citizens, all thron'd elate,

And treading each a sovran destiny,
Shall count it yet their pride and best estate
To steadily for commonwealth co-operate.

21

Who'd be the bard of that triumphant time?
Who hath the pen of promise, and the skill,
To tell its periods in exultant rhyme?
For I am but a dreamer on a hill,
And fain withal fantastic hours to fill
With fancies running wild of thought, or gloat
Eerie on the rising Moon, until
Betimes I hear her dim, harmonic note—
Boding of forbidden things and themes remote.

22

But so a passing ship—a bugle call—
Did tempt me to essay a song of State
Beyond the range of my poor art, as all
You rank'd Olympians, that loom serrate
Against the azure upper air, are great
O'er this low hill. To them young Morning throws
His golden first largesse—there, lingering late,
Rose-mantled Eve her deep allegiance shows,
Glorious 'mid unconquer'd peaks and virgin snows.

A Romance of the Lost

Fey

1

Up from a sea that was Celtic,
  On a midsummer night of old,
A fairy rose in the moonlight
  Where the swooning waters roll'd
To a crag that was crown'd with a castle,
  Irregular, round and high—
The castle bold, embattled,
  Of days gone by.

2

And a piper paced the ramparts
  In his own clan-tartan clad,
With the ancient arms accoutred
  That his father's father had;
And the pipes that he play'd were chanting
  Of valor and Highland pride—
To the tune of them kings had conquer'd,
  And heroes died.

3

Tho' only a lad come twenty,
  He could hold with any man,
And well was he taught in the music,
  And well could he lead his clan;
And the gallant air he was playing
  He played as never before—
Then he ceased and drew from its scabbard
  His bright claymore.

4

And he waved it aloft, exulting
  In the promise of coming years,
And feats of arms and glory

Got from the shock of spears—
Ah! the glint of that jewell'd claymore
  That his father's father had—
'Twill be handled with honor surely
  By that gay lad!

5

But O, my Bonnie, my Bonnie!
  What sound is this in thine ears,
That no man nor maid in the castle
  Nor drousing warder hears?
What music around thee is rising?
  What Orient notes unknown?
O out on the sea what is singing
  By the lone—by the lone?

6

In a maze he listen'd unmoving
  Thro' the long sweet summer night
To the song of the water-kelpie,
  Till the moon sank out of sight;
And the kitchen maids of the castle
  Found him at break of day,
As they thought, on the ramparts, drunken
  He was fey—he was fey!

7

And the thrall of a lordly ambition,
  And the combat for lands and gold,
And titles and trinkets of honor,
  And things that are bought and sold,
O! thereafter he held them so lightly!
  But aye as he went on his way,
Of a song he would be singing:
He was fey—he was fey!

8

The chieftain of all most gentle,
  Most ready with loyal sword,
But not in the years did he prosper,
  And he fail'd of the World's reward;
His king gave his lands to a stranger,
  And his lady was lost, they say;
And he died in a battle, forgotten—
  Well-a-day—well-a-day!

9

Comes something akin to a feeling
  That no language of men can define,
Not to one in a million revealing
  Its meaning by symbol or sign,
But told of in Sagas and olden
  Legends of longing and weir—
A sound in a silence too golden
  For many to hear.

10

Moments remote, unimagin'd,
  That come and go in a breath,
Thro' the light of long days uneventful,
  In the pallor of imminent death;
In the fire of some red revolution,
  Perchance in the tapers' shine
On some extravagant altar,—
  Some say in wine.

11

No matter, if only—if only
  That sound from the silence it brings;
That ray from the occult reunion
  Found in the finish of things;
Unfitted thereafter, exalted,

Uncaring, they pass among men,
And the World, as they knew it, is never
The same again.

12

Once, in the dull way of mortals,
　As I lay in a stupor, I felt,
As I fancied, the palpable portals
　Of darkness commingle and melt
Away into somnolent gardens,
　Hidden forever from day:
Ah! from them I never would waken,
　Could I stay—could I stay!

13

Could I dream within arbors Lethean,
　Where the poppies that nod in the night
Have yielded at last to the perfume
　Of roses enchantingly white;
Where Morphia lies, and her lore is
　Reveal'd, and her secrets are told
In fragments of fathomless stories
　Forgotten of old!

14

O souls made fit for the losing
　Of all that the World implies,
Yet who tread not the pathway of heroes,
　Nor of saints that agonize,
What vision is this that you treasure
　Like children, until you are grey?
Elusive, alluring forever,—
　You are fey—you are fey!

A Romance of the Lost

The Lost Castle

Once upon a time there stood
  A Castle by the Western sea:
Near by there was a gnomish wood
  Ancient and wild with glamorie
  Of ferly things wrought secretly:
There I was free as it were mine,
  For those who ruled were kin to me:
But the Lords o' the Castle are dead lang syne!

Oft in that wood from my old beldame
  I fled thro' hushed elf-haunted ways:
But the clatter there was when the gay Lords came
  Laughing back from their brave forays!
  Great sport they had, and high feast days,
Follow'd by long red nights of wine,
  With ball and banquet rooms ablaze:
But the Lords o' the Castle are dead lang syne!

A moment now to me it seem'd
  As if low golden bells had rung
Out of the forest where I dream'd
  Years ago when I was young:
  And even now 'twas on my tongue
To tell a tale too fair and fine
  For the like of these I dwell among:
But the Lords o' the Castle are dead lang syne!

Slow accumulating hours!
  And the last rays of the Sun shine
Redly over the ruin'd towers!
  But the Lords o' the Castle are dead lang syne!

Rhymes of a Rounder

C. CANADIAN EPICS AND NARRATIVES

Lonesome Bar

1

Out of the North there rang a cry of Gold!
And all the spacious regions of the West,
From rugged Caribou to where the crest
Of Mexicon Sièrras mark the old
Franciscan frontiers, caught the regal sound,
And echo'd and re-echo'd it, till round
The eager World the rumor of it roll'd:
How Eldorado once again was found
  Where stretch Canadian plains, forlorn and rude,
Hard upon the iron-temper'd Arctic solitude.

2

Then woke the vanguard of adventurers,
Who fret their souls against the trammel'd ways
And measur'd hours of these exacting days;
They heard the call—the pirate call that stirs
To reach for easy gold in regions new;
That once from lazy Latin cities drew
Pizarro and his pious plunderers,
And, later, many a buccaneering crew
  To sail their curly ships across the foam
And loot the Spanish galleons upon the run for home.

3

So rake the annals of the knave Romance—
The breed will not die out! The fatal stars
That sway the line of loose Irregulars
For evermore 'gainst hazard circumstance,
Illumin'd thro' those triple golden years
A trail of splendid hopes and ghastly fears,
Where only now Aurora gleams askance
On the twinkling, frosted bones of pioneers;

But ho! for savage lands alight with spoil—
For ventures grim and treasure-trove on a stark, unheard-of
      soil!

4

And I went with the crowd who took the trail
Over the icy Chilcoot; side by side
Who tugg'd and toil'd and topp'd the White Divide,
Rafted it to Tagish, and set sail
Down the rapid Yukon long before
The main rush reach'd the mines. 'Twas no more
To me than some new game of head-and-tail
To gamble on; but we drank deep, and swore,
Around uproarious campfires, that we'd find
Our fortunes on the Klondike creeks or leave our bones
      behind.

5

But there was a hoodoo on me from the first;
Tho' everywhere I saw the yellow glance
Of other's gold, I seem'd to stand no chance
Locating claims; the hot, mosquito-curst
And scurvy days went empty-handed by,
No matter what I'd do or where I'd try;
And every day in passing seem'd the worst,
Until the last day faded from the sky,
And the long, inexorable Night had come,—
Inlocked with cold, and weird stars, and dumb as a corpse is
      dumb.

6

I work'd a while that Winter on a lay;
Sixty below, and sleeping in snow-bank'd tents,—
Say, that was the hardpan of experience!
Just earning enough to live, and make a play
On some infernal card that never won;
Or easy by some dance-hall beauty done

For all the dust I had—you know the way:
Snow-blind once, once frozen to the bone,
While mushing with the mails between the creeks;
Then typhoid laid me on my back delirious for weeks.

7

The river-ice was breaking in the Spring
When first I heard them tell of Lonesome Bar,—
A haggard region hidden in the far
Blank reaches of the North past reckoning.
But the Sun was warm again, 'twas afternoon,
And I was lounging in the Log Saloon,
Ready to turn my hand to anything,
When in two strangers came with a tale that soon
Drew round the restless crowd, for ever fond
Of newer strikes, and farther fields, and the luck of things
      beyond.

8

And well within an hour the rush began,
For the strangers spoke of fortunes in a day;
Careless show'd us nuggets that would weigh
An ounce or more, and told how every man
At Lonesome Bar had sacks of them. Stampede!
Already the sleds are out, and the huskies lead,
Uneasy at their traces in the van,
And yelping 'gainst the time the packers need:
Stampede! Stampede! All hangs on the moment's haste,—
And it's every man and dog for himself on the endless Arctic
      waste!

9

But the fever shook me still in every bone;
Times I'd feel my legs bend under me,
And every sinew loosen utterly;
And so I fell behind. Yet all alone
I mush'd along for a month as best I could,

And every mile I made was to the good,
For the trail of those ahead in the bleak unknown
I'd savvy enough to keep. At last I stood
One day on a rocky bluff, outworn and weak,
And saw beneath me Lonesome Bar, at the bend of Boulder Creek.

10

All! well I mind the evening that I came!
The month was June, nigh ripen'd to July,
And the hour was midnight, yet the Western sky
From the horizontal Sun was all aflame,
When with my empty pack I sauntered down
The one long tented street that made the town,
Hungry and sick—sick of a losing game,
And broke for the price of a whiskey-straight to drown
The ragged thoughts a-limping thro' my brain—
Till I saw a crowd and went beside to hear what news again.

11

And there was a gaunt old ruffian, shaggy-brow'd,
Who on a barrel, as far as I could tell,
Ranted in drunken ecstasy of Hell!
They suited well his theme—that Klondike crowd:
Men dogg'd by shadows of despair and crime,
With women reckless of all aftertime;
Miners, traders, villains unavow'd,
And nondescript of every race and clime;
With the red police of Canada beside—
For they keep tab on everything clear down to the Arctic tide.

12

But Hell! What use had I for Hell that night?
And sullen I turned away, when I felt a whack
From a heavy open hand upon my back,
And, turning quick, my doubtful eyes caught sight
Of a college chum of mine—one Julien Roy—

Whom I'd not seen for years. Christ! 'twas joy
To see the face of him again, and, quite
In his old way, to hear him say, "Old boy!
You're down on your luck, I see! Come on up town,
Where we can talk and have something to eat, and something
    to wash it down!"

13

'Twas like the sudden shining of the Sun!
The flowers forgotten of old fellowship
Went all abloom again,—there seem'd to slip
A weight of wasted years and deeds ill-done
Plumb down and out of my life, with chance to try
The upward trail again, where he and I
Could venture yet the highest to be won,
Could let the very thought of failure die,
And weave into our lives, from ravell'd ways,
That cord of gold we talk'd about in the far-off college days.

14

For Julien was a gentleman all through;
He stak'd me then, when I had not a cent,
Braced me up and shared with me his tent,
And help'd in every way a friend could do.
As to the fortune that is ours to-day,
I stumbled on it in the chancy way
That all things come to me; I cut in two
The likeliest claim I found, ask'd Jule to stay,
And work it with me, share and share alike,—
And in a month at Lonesome Bar 'twas rank'd the richest
    strike.

15

One day I left him working on the claim,
I had to buy supplies down at the Bar,
When passing by the dance-hall Alcazar,
Topmost on its board I read a name,

"Beulah, the Singing Girl!" The lesser lights,
The Dogans, with Obesity in tights,
And the boneless Acrobat—same old game—
'Twas not for them I stay'd, nor clownish sights
But I wanted to hear a song—a song to make
The feel of younger days come back until my heart should ache.

16

Something went wrong with me that night, I know;
And yet I swear I would not set it right
For all the North and all its gold in sight!
White she was all over, like the snow
That on the glacier in the moonlight lies,
And lissome as a panther when it spies
Its quarry where the forest branches low;
But the luring of her deep-illumin'd eyes,
And voice voluptuous with all desire,
And somewhat else beyond all that fair set my soul on fire.

17

For Beulah sang a ballad to me then,
Of perilous tune, so put to velvet rime,
'Twas sure the kind that sirens in old time
Sang from the weedy rocks to sailor-men;
And all the while her eyes shone splendidly
At something far too fine for us to see;
But O! at the ending of the ballad, when
Those eyes sank down to rest alone on me,
Full well for one such glance of hers I knew
I'd tip my hat to her command for all that a man may do.

18

And so enamor'd on the instant grown,
I sprang to meet her when the song was done;
She met me wondrous kind; then one by one
The others drew aside, while we, alone,

Crush'd from the moments, in our eagerness,
A wine of many years, as one would press
Sudden the ripen'd grapes. Ah! we had known,
In some strange way that I'm too old to guess,
A dream of life between, I know not how,
That linked her alien soul to mine with a dream-outlasting vow!

19

You know how goes the custom of the Camp;
How swift the wooing where the pace is set
To live all in the hour—and then forget!
The midnight moon shone pale, like an onyx lamp
Hung in the amber twilight of the sky,
When we went forth together, she and I,
And open'd yellow wine, whose yellow stamp
Won high approval from the rascals dry
Who pledg'd us o'er and o'er, upon the chance
To waste in regions barbarous that vintage of old France.

20

The first ones of the North still tell of it:
That was the night the Lucky Swede made bold
To bid for Beulah all her weight in gold;
And when, from mere caprice, my side she quit,
And challenged him to make the offer good,
With iron pans and a beam and a chunk of wood
A rough-and-ready balance soon was fit,
And the Swede brought up his gold where Beulah stood,
And 'gainst her weight upon the other scale
He piled his buckskin-sacks, while I—saw red, but watch'd the sale.

21

In all my life I never felt so broke;
But when the balance quiver'd evenly,
She threw a kiss to him—and came to me,

And my heart went all a-tremble as she spoke:
"Olè, you're a sport all right—for a Swede!
But I think this Sourdough here's the man I need;
I only play'd to leave him for a joke;
Let's call it off—and the drinks on me! Agreed?"
Since then for me there's been no other girl—
And all the boys shook hands on it, and things began to whirl.

22

And it's something worth, even in memory,
To linger thro' those ample hours again.
It may not be the same with other men,
But clear on the topmost waves of revelry
The soul of me was lifted cool and clean,
Silent—to feel the surge of what had been:
Content—to weigh the evil yet to be:—
Then Beulah's arms closed warm and white between,
And I let go of all in her embrace,
And for a time escaped from time and the latitudes of space.

23

And the last was a sense of sound—a tremulo,
So vagrant, sweet and low, 'twas like the thin,
Continual twinkling tune of a mandolin
To mellow-toned guitars in Mexico,
Where lovers pace the plaza by the sea;
Where the deep Pacific phosphorescently
Goes rolling smoothly 'neath the Moon, as tho'
The influence of her yellow witchery
Thro' all the sparkling waters off the Main
Had sunken, sunken, drunken down like limitless champagne.

24

Slowly I woke. The last of the stars had fled:
Only beside me Beulah murmur'd "Stay!"
And kiss'd me, sleepy-eyed. But early day
Chills all of that somehow; I turned instead,

Thinking to leave her dreaming, I confess;
Yet even in that grey light her loveliness,
And certain drowsy, dulcet words she said,
Charm'd my heart to hers in a last caress—
Chained if you like, and clinch'd with a parting smile—
What then? In the round of the World I've found naught else
      so well worth while.

25

Far up a valley, where the summer-rills
Long ages thro' the glacial-drift have roll'd,
I work'd in gravel studded thick with gold
For days and days on the double-shift that kills.
Yet oft, to hear the echoes ring and stir
That vacant valley like a dulcimer,
I flung her name against the naked hills,
And crimson'd all the air with thoughts of her;
While 'mong the fair returning stars I'd see
Pale phantoms of her chill, sweet face receding endlessly,

26

Till I could stand the pull of it no more;
I, who as a fool knew every phase
Of woman's lighter love, and love's light ways,
Had felt no passion like to this before.
As the lost drunkard's longing at its worst,
And keen as the craving of the opium-curst,
Was the elemental lust that overbore
My very body till it gasp'd athirst,
As one in some fierce desert dying dreams
Of snowy peaks and valleys green with unavailing streams.

27

And Julien, good old Julien, knowing all,
Pretended not to know, but said he guess'd
That I had overwork'd myself, and best
Lay off a spell in town. Then I let fall

My useless tools, and wash'd and got in trim
For the long ten miles ahead. The trail was slim,
And crawl'd at times 'gainst some sheer granite wall,
Or lost itself 'mong boulders huge and grim;
But dreaming of her I pick'd a buoyant way,
Descending easy to the Bar at ending of the day.

28

That region was abandon'd years ago,
And Lonesome Bar is to the wild again,
Yet still it haunts me as I saw it then:—
Far up in the banner'd West a crimson glow,
And a silver crescent on its edge aslant,
With jewell'd Venus sinking jubilant
Thro' opal spaces of the vault below;
Then goblin rocks and waterfalls and scant
Green tamarac around the white marquee
Where Beulah lodg'd—and there was ending of the trail for me.

29

Ending of the trail—for she was there!
Sylph-like I saw her figure thro' the haze
Made of the twilight and the camp-fire blaze;
And the piney odors passing thro' the air
So pure I took for random kisses blown
From her red mouth to mine, while yet unknown
My whereabouts; then wholly unaware
I stole upon her standing there alone,
And sudden she was mine without appeal,
And lip to lip within my arms made all my fancies real.

30

Shall I forget the words she said to me?
Nay, I believ'd them—I believe them yet!
She told me how she dream'd that we had met
Where dreams are true; and then how endlessly,

Like some lost dove, she roamed this evil world
Seeking for me; how now her wings were furl'd,
And I should bide with her, till I should see
This whitest secret in her soul impearl'd;
And her songs were all for me, I heard her say,—
For me, for me and only me, forever and a day!

31

Then pass'd the last good hours I ever knew;
I lit my pipe, sat on a log, and look'd
At her and her neat hands that neatly cook'd
A supper hot and homely—just for two;
And out in God's sweet air, beside the fire,
Where comrade ways but strengthen'd Love's desire,
We made it up to marry then for true,
And I thought how all my life I'd never tire
Of loving her, her eyes, her voice, her form,
Her charm of something unreveal'd for ever young and warm.

32

But at last, as night drew on, she rose and said:
"I'd talk with you till dawn, dear, if talk
Could hold my audience or charm the clock,
But I musn't miss my turn, so come ahead!"
Down at the theatre the crowd was thin,
Perhaps two score, no more, as we went in;
But the manager was hanging out his red
Big-letter'd signal-lantern to begin,
When from the street, crescendo, came a roar,
Nearer and still nearer, till it reach'd the dance-hall door.

33

Beulah stood ready on the stage, and the black
Professor at the crack'd piano play'd
His overture twice through, but no one stay'd,
So I joined in where all were crowding back
To where the row was on. "Speech, Mac, speech!"

They cried, as up the aisle they rush'd to reach
Where Beulah stood, confused. "It's Hellfire Mac!"
I whisper'd her, "and he's drunk and wants to preach!"
"What! why sure—whoever he is—come, dear,
That lets me off for a while, you know; come on—come on in here!"

34

And laughing softly she drew me aside
Into a rough alcove, her dressing-room,
Curtain'd from the stage, and half in gloom,
When at a sound her eyes 'gan staring wide,
And she clutch'd my arm. 'Twas not the pious drone,
But a fearsome something in the undertone
Of the ruin'd Calvinist, whose soul espied
Damnation toppling from the great White Throne
Upon the woeful habiters of Earth,
That somehow check'd the crowd that night, and still'd its shallow' mirth.

35

And Beulah, more than all like one enthrall'd,
Smother'd a moan, and dumbly motioning
For me to follow, crept into the wing
Close up to him. Bearded, grey and bald,
With eyes sunk gleaming under beetling shag,
And face rough-chisel'd like a granite crag,
He tower'd above us all; but so appall'd
He seem'd that scarce his drunken tongue could drag
Meet words to match his ghastly fantasies,
Yet I remember some in Gaelic accents drawn like these:

36

"Last night, my friens, she dreampt she was a snake,
Prodigious as wass nefer seen before:
Ha, ta Mac an Diaoul!—ta Peishta-Mor!
For when she moved she made ta mountains quake,

And all ta waters of ta oceans roll
In frightnet waves from Pole to frozen Pole;
While efermore her starving body'd ache
So bitterly ta pain she couldna thole,
But twistit round and round, till she was curl'd
In endless coils of blastit flesh about ta blastit World.

37

"For in those days she was ta only thing;
There wass no man nor woman left at all;
No fish to swim, no beast to run or crawl,
No bird nor butterfly to spread its wing;
Around ta world herself wass all alone,
For all that efer lived to her had grown;
And Winter, that would nefermore be Spring,
Now glowert silent ofer every zone:
Then liftit she her head into ta sky
To spit ta last great blasphemy into God's face—and die.

38

"But O! ta silence of ta endless sky—
And O! ta blackness of ta endless Night!
Where all ta stars can nefer make it light—
Where in ta empty, like a Defil's eye,
Ta eerie Sun, grown small and smooth and cold,
Stared down upon her doom ordain'd of old!
And she torment—and she couldna tell for why—
With agonies in every quaking fold,
Where only flowit poison streams for blood:
And still she hiss'd and spit and curst—and still there wass no
        God!

39

"But at ta last she felt ta power to make
Ta great escape, and finish all her hurt;
Ta Spirit moved her, and her body girt
Its straining coils until ta World she brake

To splinter'd rocks that ground and crash'd and roar'd,
While all ta inner fires reek'd up and pour'd
In fury round ta universal Snake—
Consuming in ta vengeance of ta Lord!"
We never heard the meaning of his dream,
For sudden thro' the building rang a wild hysteric scream.

40

And Beulah springing frenzied to the stage,
And the old man halting face to face with her,
Too swift and strange for any theatre
Follow'd a scene whose measure none could gauge,
Only we felt its mad reality.
"That man's my father—keep him back from me!"
I heard her cry, while horror blent with rage
Upon the other's face. "A fient I see!
A damit fient of Hell, who stole my name!
Beulah, ta harlot, come again to cross my face with shame!"

41

I saw the old man grip and throttle her;
I saw her choking, and her white hand dart
Down to the knife that flashed—and found his heart!
I saw him reel and fall—I saw the blur
Of blood that gush'd upon her heaving breast
Out of his own! Ah! God, how quick the rest!
Ere I or any one of us could stir,
Full to the hilt that fatal knife she press'd
Into her side, that ran and reek'd with red,
As she fell dead upon the stage where lay her father dead.

42

Moments there are that gleam beyond all Time!
Blown from enormous Years! O name that seems
To hearken back thro' vague primeval dreams!
O maid remember'd from the young, sublime,
Untrammel'd days when God foregathered us!

My woman still—grown strangely perilous!
All in a moment marr'd with scarlet crime,
And lost before mine eyes incredulous!
My woman still—tho' I go babbling, dazed
At thought of her and her father damn'd, and a Hell of things gone crazed!

43

How since that hour again and yet again
I've play'd the fool with Death! Go let him take
What shape he please, I'll meet him wide awake,
And keep a date with him—no matter when!
Mad, I tell you—mad, I've laughed to hear
In Winter-time the mad grey wolves draw near
And circle round me, all unarm'd—and then,
Snapping their teeth, slink back and howl with fear:
God knows of what! So queer it seem'd, almost
I think they saw beside me there old Hellfire's drunken ghost!

44

Lonesome Bar! Too far—too far and old
The hollow sound of it now comes to me
To quicken this sick heart that crazily
Goes lurching on to everlasting cold!
Fill up my glass! What game have I to play
But drink into this drear, indifferent day,
Some brief delirium, wherein to hold
A phantom floating goldenly away
Beyond the zenith of my soul, as bright
Aurora with her dreamlight haunts the hopeless Arctic night!

A Romance of the Lost

ANTHOLOGY

The Rhyme of Jacques Valbeau

1

One August afternoon I saw,
Somewhere back of Ottawa,
   Among the oldest hills,
A young and most alluring squaw,
Togg'd in a buckskin petticoat,
   With buckskin fringe and frills:
Catamount-claws were at her throat,
   Fixt on a catgut string,
With copper beads and color'd quills,—
   O she was the dreamliest thing!
Clean and cool as the dews that cling
To the tiger-lilies on those hills
   Thro' the golden August dawns;
For the rest—the sunlight gleam'd
On breasts and arms and legs that seemed
Moulded brownly out of bronze:
Shapely, slender, debonair,
From her coils of blue-black hair
To her dainty moccasins:
And I met her, for my sins,
Somewhere back of Ottawa,
   Among the oldest hills.

2

Long ago in the earlies
A Frenchman lived in France:
Gaunt he was like an eagle,
With an evil, eagle glance:
One eye was black and one was blue,
And the black one look'd straight into you,
   While the blue one leer'd askance,
   Most sinfully in Paris.
But it was wiser not to try
   To hinder him or harass,

But quietly to pass him by,
  In the sinful streets of Paris;
For his arm was strong, and his sword was long,
  And when he made sword-plays,
'Twas hard to look him in the eye,
  Because he look'd two ways;
The black one look'd straight into you,
And the blue one where he'd pink you through,
And that was a trick entirely new
  To people then in Paris.
O he had small fears of the musketeers
  Or the macaroons of Paris!
And he had his time, and he made most free,
And he lived in great ribalderie,
  In the sinful streets of Paris.
But at last those evil eyes in his head
On whom they fell, or so 'tis said,
  Brought such annoy and harass,
That when King Louis heard of it,
  He order'd him from Paris:
Yes; not for the evil life he led,
  Nor the ways that he walk'd unfit,
But for those two evil eyes in his head,
They press'd him out of Paris.

3

'Twas long ago in the earlies,
And he thought to take a chance
For fortune in the fur-trade,
So he sail'd away from France,
In a crooked ship, with a crooked deck,
That sprang a leak and went to wreck
Five hundred miles from our Quebec,
  At the mouth of our Saint Lawrence.
How then he fared I do not know,
'Twas long ago, but this is so,
That up the river, paddling slow,

Half-starv'd, at length he reach'd Quebec,
And told his tale of dismal wreck,—
His name was Jacques Valbeau.
Now in those days in our Quebec
  Nigh all the folk were pious,
And when they saw his one black eye,
  With the blue one on the bias,
They cross'd themselves, and wish'd the rogue
  Had drown'd 'tween there and Paris.
Yet money is made in the fur-trade,
  When others hunt the fur,
And some thought best that they should test
  This lank adventurer;
And so they offer'd to subscribe
Enough to outfit and equip
Jacques Valbeau for a hunting trip
  With some of the Huron tribe.
Thus did he go, this Jacques Valbeau,
And for many days he studied the ways
  And the words of the Huron tribe.

4

Yes; money is made in the fur-trade
  When others hunt the fur,
But brandy to the Indians
  If you want the best of fur,
And everything else they have to show;
'Tis a law you know, and Jacques Valbeau
  Was its discoverer.
So for many days he studied the ways
  And words of every tribe.
Of money had he not a sou markee,
  But he carried a bottled bribe,
And the Moon turn'd round, and he prosper'd some,
  With beaver-skins and such,
That he got for his brandy, and then for rum,
  And the gin of the heretic Dutch.

But me it would take too long to describe
How things went bad in every tribe
   Which the Church had held in check;
But sure there was trouble plenty too much
   In our dear old Quebec.
So the Bishop and the Governor,
   Who sometimes did agree,
They met and talk'd the matter o'er,
   And settled finally
That they would have this Jacques Valbeau
   And hang him by the neck
Up on the windy citadel
   Of our dear old Quebec.
But so it is, and so it is,
   And one can never tell,
For in the Garden Ursuline
That evil-eyed Valbeau had seen
An Indian girl turned seventeen,
   A sweet young sauvagesse,
Left with the Lady Prioress
To learn to sew, and cook nice food,
And tell her beads, and to confess,
   And otherwise be good.
But Jacques Valbeau, that Jacques Valbeau,
   He signalled her so well
In forest ways she understood,
   That just at vesper-bell
Of that same evening long ago
She slipt away into the wood:—
O wicked Jacques Valbeau!

5

So Jacques took to the wilderness,
   The first coureur-de-bois,
And with him went that Indian girl,
   Whose convent-name was Lottilà—
   With the accent on the "aw."

I have heard her other name, but now
  I will not try to tell it,
Because I can't, and 'cause there are
  No letters that will spell it.
But O, 'twas the good, good time they had
  Thro' the woods in the summer weather!
Hunting and fishing and trading in furs,
  And they were so rich together,
Until one night as they lay asleep,
Where the moss was growing thick and deep,
  'Gainst the trunk of a fallen tree,
The Iroquois Indians silently
  Began to creep and creep
In a closing circle where they lay,
Till scarce they were more than three yards away.
Then a twig did snap with a warning crack;
Upsprang that valiant rover, Jacques,
All in an instant wide awake,
And three of those Iroquois heads did break
  Before they had him down. Alack!
They tied his hands behind his back
  And fixt him to a stake;
And his bottles of Jamaica rum
  They drank till they were drunk.
And then the squaws began to plunk
With rattly sticks on the big tum-tum,
That's a sort of Indian drum,
And the braves a ring did make
And danced around him at that stake
  The while the squaws did squawk;
They danced around him at that stake,
With painted cheek and feathered head,
Each swinging a horrible tomahawk
  And gum-stick burning red,
And told him how his scalp they'd take,
And otherwise keep him awake
Until the hungry day should break,
  Then cut him into blocks

And finally his body bake,
When sure that it no more could ache,
And eat his heart when he was dead:
Of these details perhaps I've said
   Too much—the subject shocks.

6

But so it is, and so it is,
   And one can never tell;
For on Valbeau the flesh did sizz,
   And he began to yell,
When the Devil, moving mightily
   Somewhere down in Hell,
Did cause a terrible earthquake,
And all of Canada did shake
From Ottawa to Rimouski.
(This happen'd in sixteen sixty-three,
And it's all set out in history.)
But Jacques Valbeau stood swarthily,
   And desperate at the stake,
And called the Devil to his aid,
While all the Indians, dismay'd,
Took to their naked knees and pray'd,
And the ground kept heaving heavily.
Yes, all took to their knees and pray'd,
But Lottilà, the little squaw,
Who, with no thought but her lover's life,
Cut thro' his thongs with a scalping-knife,
While the ground kept heaving heavily.
And then was that great bargain made
As Jacques Valbeau stood swarthily;
He call'd the Devil to his aid,
And the Devil, moving mightily
   Somewhere down in Hell,
Roar'd reply, so I am told,
That Jacques Valbeau, the overbold,
   And Lottilà as well,

If they would do his will alway,
Should laugh at Time and never grow old,
And none should hinder them or check,
Whether at work or whether at play,
Free to come and free to go
Thro' all the Province of Quebec
And the borders of Ontario—
   Down to the Judgment Day!

7

Then Jacques Valbeau and Lottilà,
So the Iroquois declare
(And I have cause to think 'tis true),
While others crouch'd all in despair,
Follow'd a ball of fire that ran
Down to the river near St. Anne,
   Till it stopt by a big canoe;
And Lottilà she fainted there,
   And fell in that big canoe,
And Jacques, half dead, he fell there too.
Then it rose of itself in the spectral air,
   And far out of sight it flew.
How long it was they never knew,
It may have been days, but Jacques came to,
And found they were still in the big canoe,
Hovering over a landscape fair,
   Late in the afternoon.
And it floated aimless, here and there,
But Jacques Valbeau had ready wit,
And he sat and consider'd the matter a bit,
   Till with a paddle soon
He caught the trick of sailing it,
Slowly at first and cautiously,
But at last he sail'd as joyously
   As any bird on the wing;
While Lottilà woke up to sing
   To the end of the afternoon.

Then a down-worn mountain they did see,
   From whose green covering
The granite ribs sagg'd outwardly;
It seem'd some monstrous ancient thing
   Crouching wearily.
But on its summit they did light,
And make their camp there for the night;
In later days, upon that site,
   But lower down the hill,
Jacques built a cabin large and strong,
And near to it a whiskey-still
   To make the whiskey-blanc.
And more I'd like to tell to you
Of how he did the Devil's will
   In that bewitch'd canoe,
But the tale of it would be too long,
   O much too long, indeed!
Yet in parish-records you may read
How, with a drunken shanty-crew,
They saw him pass in that canoe,
Piercing the clouds with awful speed,—
   Let that be a lesson to you!

8

So thus that August afternoon,
   Among those haunted hills,
I met that young, bedevill'd squaw,
The luring, lissome Lottilà,
   Minding her whiskey-stills.
And truly I was glad I met her,
Yet I am shy, and sometimes nervous,
And I wonder'd what excuse would serve us
   To know each other better;
But lifting my hat to the brown, young maid,
She smiled straight at me, unafraid,
   And presently began
To speak with pretty words that ran

Thro' English, French and Indian,—
　　It was a lovely jargon;
But she said no word of Jacques Valbeau,
Who with the Devil, long ago,
　　Made such a splendid bargain;
　　So how was I to know?
Now it's sometimes sweet to be indiscreet,
As for me I am never wise;
So we sat us down on the warm, dry sod,
'Mid brown grass and golden rod,
　　Watching the butterflies.
And she talk'd and talk'd as I held her hand,
And when I could not understand
I look'd down deep into her eyes.
　　Perhaps the thing sounds silly,
But think of the picture that she made,
　　Array'd like a tiger-lily:
Her body brown and quivering
In that revealing petticoat,
With catamount-claws at her fine throat
　　Fixt on a catgut string;
And the copper beads and color'd quills,
Just that and her dainty moccasins,—
　　O she was the dreamliest thing!
And I met her, for my sins,
Somewhere back of Ottawa,
　　Among the oldest hills.

9

The sun was slipping down the sky,
　　Close to the green horizon,
When sudden I saw the fairiest sight
　　That ever I set my eyes on:
A yellow canoe, with three of a crew,
　　Almost too fast to follow,
Straight out of the sky to the hilltop nigh,
　　Came skimming along like a swallow;

And then to the cabin, right below,
It slid with a motion easy and slow,
And a man stept out—already you know
'Twas Jacques Valbeau—'twas Jacques Valbeau!
  Gaunt he was like an eagle,
  With an evil, eagle glance;
His black eye look'd me through and through,
  And his blue one leer'd askance;
The front of his head had been tomahawk'd,
  But part way down his back,
His hair was flowing coarse and black,
  Like the tail of a horse that is dockt;
But he had a very engaging smile,
  And I liked the way that he talk'd.
He was straight as an arrow when he walk'd,
  And, after a little while,
I thought him a handsome man—almost,
And really, quite a delightful host.
He introduced the other two
Who rode with him in the big canoe.
One was a fat little country girl,
With carroty hair in a towsell'd curl,
Her dolly eyes had tears at the rim,
And her face was pale as milk that is skim,
  And she was a sad little girl.
The other guest was a shantyman,
  Half drunk by the looks of him;
But the shantyman was an Irishman,
  And that is enough for him.
Then Lottilà and the country girl
  Left us and went to the upper
Cabin above the whiskey-still,
  To set the table for supper,
While we sat down in the red sunlight,
  And listened to Jacques Valbeau
  As he told prodigious stories
  Of two hundred years ago,
Of all the old coureurs-de-bois

Dead so long ago,—
   We still there in the red sunlight,
   And they all underground.
Then I heard a sound, and I look'd around,
   Then up where Lottilà
Was ringing a queer little oblong bell—
   (Maybe 'twas just a cowbell,
Tho' I think 'twas silver, so clear and sweet
   The silver tone of it fell) —
And gladly we follow'd Valbeau to the upper
Cabin where we were to have our supper.
For me, I was more than ready to eat,
   And the supper was a dream.
We'd buttermilk and new potat,
And a roasted chicken, great and fat,
   With cauliflower in cream,
And a glass or two of whiskey-blanc,
Just to help the meal along,
And another glass, and after that
   Tabac de habitant.

10

Upon my soul, I never knew
Just when we enter'd the big canoe,
The same as one can never keep
The moment clear one falls asleep.
But so it was until I found
We were no more upon the ground.
Now I at times am extremely nervous,
As I said before, and when I found
How that bewitch'd canoe did swerve us
Up and away from the solid ground,
With the hills a-sinking all around,
And we once more in the copper glim
Of the Sun we lost somewhile before,
O then, indeed, I thought small blame
To the frighten'd girl with the towsell'd curl,

And dolly eyes with tears at the rim,
And face all pale as milk that is skim—
   I'll bet that my own was the same!
But the shantyman was too drunk, I think,
To know where we were—it's a beastly shame
   The way those Irish drink.

11

Now remember aviation
Differs quite from navigation,
For always in the water
Of the river that you ride in,
Or be it smooth or ripply,
A canoe is very tipply,
And steadily you kneel.
But through the air you glide in
A fashion that you feel
It's a medium to confide in,
And you needn't keep a keel,—
That much I saw at a glance.
And tho' I'm not sufficiently wise
To make it clear, you can't capsize
   So long as you properly balance,
   Or rise by levitation.
Now, that's why aviation
Differs quite from navigation,
And I had begun to feel easy again,
   And ready to take a chance,
When all of a sudden it started to rain
Right over our heads, and there was a growl
   Of thunder far down in the West.
Then the Sun went out, and the wind 'gan howl,
And a storm came bounding along on the crest
Of the massy clouds, grown sulphurous,
And there was the blue zig-zag and flash
Of lightning, follow'd by instant crash
   Of the thunder nearing us.

With that Valbeau began to sing,
While Lottilà did sway and swing
  Her brown arms perilous:
    Gai faluron falurette,
      Gai faluron dondé!
I did the same but tremblingly,
And the Indian girl did grin with glee
  To see the white girl, shrunk,
With her face in her hands and her head on my knee,
  But the shantyman still lay drunk,
  So how could I put her away?
  It was all so characteristic!
    Gai faluron falurette,
      Gai faluron dondé!
Now, it's all very fine to sing that way
  When everything else is right,
But we sailed straight into a loaded cloud,
  So villainous anarchistic
It bang'd like tons of dynamite:—
For a time I was blind with the awful light,
  And deaf with the awful roar;
I felt we were blown clean out of sight,
  And then I felt we had sunk
To the bottomless pit for evermore;
  But the shantyman still lay drunk.
It makes me shiver to think of it now,
But after a bit I rallied somehow.
Valbeau was laughing at the bow,
  And he went far back to speak:
  "Holà, monsieur; comment ça va?"
To keep my face with Lottilà,
  I managed just to stammer:
  "Bully, Valbeau—c'est magnifique!
  But go where the clouds are calmer!"

12

We were up in a cool, sweet air,
   Under a wonderful sky,
Velvety dark and richly sown
With wonderful stars from zone to zone,
   And all of them seem'd so nigh,
But a little more, and we would play
Near the opal arch of the Milky Way,
   With the yellow Moon near by.
Then over the rim we look'd far down
   Where the World had vanish'd in ire,
Where fold on fold of the black clouds roll'd,
   Roaring and fearful with fire,
And we rose from that Devil's crucible,
Like souls that are rising released from Hell,
   To regions of glory and gold.
   Higher and higher and higher!
   And the air grew thin and cold:
   But higher and higher and higher
   I urged Valbeau to explore
Nearer and nearer that border of gold
   And limit where mortals expire:
   Higher and higher and higher!
While a million millions miles to the fore,
I watch'd the glint of a jewell'd door
   In the Gardens of Desire:
   Higher and higher and higher!
Till I was dazed and my breath was gone,
   And I could see no more.

13

When I came to myself we were sailing down,
   And circling like a feather
In a slow, descending, spiral flight
   Thro' mellow moonlit weather:
And the country girl croon'd with delight,
   And claspt her hands together.

But still her head droop'd on my knee
   As she claspt her hands together,
And so close were we that none could see
   As I fool'd with a carroty curl:
Alas! I admit my conduct was raw,
For my heart was all to Lottilà,
   But I kissed the other girl.
Now it's a great mistake, when up in the skies,
   To kiss the other girl,
Just for a pair of dolly eyes,
   Or a cute little carroty curl:
Yet not the slightest harm was meant,
With me it's a matter of temperament;
   But the shantyman woke up!
   O, blast that Irish pup!
He woke and caught us in the act,
Just at the moment our lips had smackt,
And he went for me, hell-bent;
Let out from his ugly throat a yell,
Told Lottilà just what he saw,
   And—before I had time to explain,
   Or argue against the fact—
   That fact so apparently plain—
They both made at me so savage I fell
   Without a chance to prepare!
And I fell, and I fell, and I fell—my Lord!
It's the awfulest feel to fall overboard
   From a canoe away up in the air:
It's really too swift to describe or tell,
But first you feel you're out of it,
   And then you feel a thump,
And after that you're generally
   A most unlovely lump.
But in my case 'twas different,
My body was caught by a wind-current,
   And it drove me sideways on,
With a muffled whack, 'gainst a big haystack,
And I tumbled it over and lay on my back

Unconscious till the dawn,
  And so flat, flat, flat,
That when I arose in misery,
  A long time after that,
'Twas hard to remember where I was at,
  And I sigh'd lugubriously,
With my body so stiff and my head so sore,
It couldn't have hurt me any more
If I'd been out all night on a spree—
    Gee!

14

Now let me end, O bulbous friend!
  This rhyme ere I begin to
Tell other things irrelevant
Of venturings extravagant
  And mystery and sin too:
For I've had my time in every clime
  The Lord has led me into:—
But give me August, after all,
If I be free to roam and loll
Among those tiger-lily hills
  Back of Ottawa.
I am ready to risk whatever befall
To meet once more that little squaw,
The luring lissome Lottilà,
  Minding her whiskey-stills;
To listen again to her pretty patois,
And hold her hand and hear her sing
Among those tiger-lily hills,
  For she was the dreamliest thing!
    Gai faluron falurette,
  I think I hear her yet.
Out there, in her buckskin petticoat,
With catamount-claws at her fine throat,
  Fixt on a catgut string;
And the copper beads and color'd quills,

And dainty moccasins,—
The girl who met me, for my sins,
Somewhere back of Ottawa,
The wanton town of Ottawa,
　Among the oldest hills.
　　Gai faluron falurette,
　　　Gai faluron dondé!

A Romance of the Lost

The Chilcoot Pass

1

Far up the Chilcoot Heights! The solid snow,
Avalanch'd from Titan peaks that rise
In stony isolation 'gainst the skies,
Hath whelm'd all in soundless overthrow;
And almost now the white and crusted mass
Hath choked the glacier's ghastly blue crevasse
That cleaves to everlasting cold below:
The wintry day declines; and down the Pass,
Where Time hath fallen, desolate, asleep,
To mark the flight of Arctic hours gigantic shadows creep.

2

But see! Upon that perilous, meagre trail,
There winding upward to a dazzling crest,
A miner inward-bound on Fortune's quest!
And tho' the sunlight's slanting weak and pale,
Tho' in the livid clouds a tempest lours,
And far above him yet the Summit towers,
He sees therein no sight to make him quail;—
'Gainst any steep he'd pit his stubborn powers;
He goes, as dauntless men have gone of old,
To play with Death in a land unknown for a stake of love and
    gold.

3

Steady he's toil'd for hours; at last he makes
A moment's pause to shift his heavy pack,
The twisted straps chafe sore upon his back,
And with hard travel all his body aches.
But now it is he notes with some dismay
What little measure's left him of the day,
And how the air's ablur with thin, white flakes;
Yet up the Pass he takes one quick survey,

Then grimly on he goes with hastening stride,
For he must be over the Summit by night—he will sleep on the other side.

4

Let others lag; he'll on with the first of the rush!
Down rivers roaring into deserts bleak,
He'll pioneer his way to the richest creek—
He'll cut and thaw the frozen earth—he'll crush
Its hoarded treasure out—and he'll call his claim
"The Little Annie!" For him that simple name
Lights up a dream of home returning flush
With store of yellow gold and golden fame;
Bringing back the happy days once more
To a little girl left lonely on the lone Lake Erie shore.

5

The gloom is deepening where the sunlight was;
The flakes are falling faster now around;
Far off he hears a shrill, foreboding sound,
And at its challenge makes another pause.
Awhile irresolute, with anxious eye,
He gazes at the menace of the sky,
And from its hue reluctant warning draws:
The storm is nigh—he little dreams how nigh—
When cursing his labor lost he turns to go
Down again for shelter to the cabin far below.

6

Save your curses, man! You walk o'erbold!
You go too slow and sullen down that path!
You may not live and brave the coming wrath
In those tumultuous clouds above you roll'd!
Save your curses, man!—for now you'll need
Every breath your body has for speed;
E'en now the air is struck with deathlier cold;
E'en now the foremost furious winds are freed;

Look!—look above you there at last,
And see the Heavens whirling downward, vague and white
    and vast!

7

So—he knows!—too late, alas, he knows
His fierce pursuers, and with desperate leap
Goes plunging madly down the uncertain steep—
Down for his life! Frantic now, he throws
His dragging pack away—his senses swim
With swift descent—the storm's o'ertaking him—
The drift in stinging clouds around him blows
To make him gasp and choke—his eyes grow dim—
Unto his very bones the cold he feels;—
But down and down that fatal Pass, tho' dazed he leaps and
    reels!

8

Far up the Chilcoot Heights! The storm is on:
He's struggling still, but now he's lost the trail,
And all his sturdy muscles flag and fail,
'Mid swirling snow, to shapes fantastic drawn
That pass like endless fleeing ghosts; and each,
In passing, seems to hiss at him and reach
Long throttling fingers out; sight is gone,
For his eyes see only white; hark! the screech
Of Arctic winds swift leaping from the sky
Down like the souls of famish'd wolves—"O Annie, lass!—
    good-bye!

9

"For now I'm play'd right out—I'm freezing fast—
I'm on the spot where I'll for ever lie,
Just when I thought my chance had come— good-bye!
Good-bye! my life is over now and past!
And it's been no use, tho' I've tried everywhere
To do the best I could, and do it square,

God's kept his grudge against me to the last,
And I've stood it now so long, I hardly care!
Let Him finish me up, right here, if He likes, and hurl
What's left of me to Hell!—But you!— O Annie— my orphan girl!"

10

White, white, white—all 'round 'tis white—
Blind white and cold;—unheard is hurl'd
His last appeal 'gainst this relentless World:
No rescue now may come—no swift respite:
The minutes of his life are almost o'er.
He knows it well;—see, he moves no more!
Body and soul can make no further fight,
Bewilder'd in the blizzard's maddening roar;
But he's facing it—he's standing rigid there—
Defying Heaven's utmost wrath in reason-rack'd despair!

11

"Blow, then, damn you—blow! You've taken all!
You—whatever Thing you are that hears—
You've never once let up on me for years!
You've stript me stark and bare as a wooden doll!
And there's not a rag of comfort left! You've blown
Every joy and every hope I've known
Roughly from my life! And when I fall,
You'll howl above me, dying here alone!
Pile on—pile on, with your blasted, strangling snow!
You can take no more but my life now! Blow! God damn you—blow!"

12

White, white, white,—unceasing white!
See! he totters, yielding to his doom—
The snow hath ready made his shroud and tomb:
But what is that? There breaks a sudden light
That startles him to last delirious cries;—

Pinnacled athwart the awful skies,
Behold a treasure-lode, uncovered bright
In transient glory to his dying eyes!
On a towering peak the sunset clouds unroll'd,
And he's gasping at the cruel splendor— "Gold—gold—gold!"

13

Far up the Chilcoot Heights! A prostrate form,
Half-buried now and motionless, doth lie
All free of pain—and, happily, to die.
Listen! He's muttering thro' the passing storm:
"Home again, Annie—home again!
God! but it's restful—after that rattling train!
It's all so still and sunny here—and so warm!
How was it I came so soon? I can't explain—
Only I know I'm home; and O! it seems
Too good to be true! Doesn't it, lass? And it's finer than all my dreams!

14

"You've grown so pretty since I've been away—
So tall and pretty—I almost seem to see
Your mother smiling there again at me,
Just like she look'd upon her wedding-day!—
A year before they laid her 'neath the grass,
And left me only you, my little lass!
Come closer to me—things grow dull and grey;—
My eyes were hurt in a blizzard on the Pass
The year I went away and left you, Pet!
What's making it dark so early, Annie? Surely it's not night yet?

15

"O! well—no matter! Whatever time it be,
I'm one of the lucky ones, I've made my pile,
And I'm going to take it easy for awhile.
No more work or worry now for me;

I've lots of gold—as yellow as your curls;
And I'll dress you fine again like the other girls,
And get you everything you want—you'll see!
A ring like mother had—and a collar of pearls;—
And I'll buy—I'll buy the old home back— that they sold!
But it's made your daddy old, dear—it's made him feel so old!

16

"Yes, I hear you laughing at me now!
But O! it's good to hear you laugh again!
To have you near and have you laugh—and then,
I must look kind of funny, I'll allow;
These clothes of mine are all so patch'd and queer!
But I'll have better ones to-morrow, dear;—
And I know you love your old dad, anyhow!
I feel so tired, I think I'll sleep just here:—
Kiss me, Annie!—there—good-night, my lass!"
God rest the souls of the dead who lie on the Heights of the Chilcoot Pass!

A Romance of the Lost

D. YOUTH/OLD

October

When I was a little fellow, long ago,
   The season of all seasons seemed to me
   The Summer's afterglow and fantasy—
The red October of Ontario:
To ramble unrestrain'd where maples grow
   Thick-set with butternut and hickory,
   And be the while companion'd airily
By elfin things a child alone may know!

And how with mugs of cider, sweet and mellow,
   And block and hammer for the gather'd store
   Of toothsome nuts, we'd lie around before
The fire at nights, and hear the old folks tell o'
   Red Indians and bears, and the Yankee war—
Long ago, when I was a little fellow!

A Romance of the Lost

Lone Wolf Lament

Drink if you will to happy days
   And things to be—but say,
Where are the fellows I used to know?
   Where are my friends to-day?

     Wow! Hear me howl!
For Shad and Pete and George and Jack
Who took the long trail and left no track:
O, never a one of them all comes back,
     And the winter-time is here!
     Wow! Hear me howl!
For Olive and June and white Irene,
And the Mexican Kid and little Corinne:
Daughters of joy who have not been seen
     This many and many a year!
I'm a lone old wolf, and I've lost my pack,
     And the winter-time is here:
     Wow! Hear me howl!

Many are gay and many are fair,
   And some still come at my call:
But I've gone lame, and can run no more,
   So what's the use of it all?

I dreamed last night I ran with them
   Under a gold-red sky,
Where the mountains rose from the green prairie—
   And I woke and wisht to die.

Drink if you will, and drink on me!
   But this is the toast I give:
Live hard with your pack and live yourselves out—
   Then ask no more to live.

     Wow! Hear me howl!
For Shad and Pete and George and Jack

Who took the long trail and left no track:
O, never a one of them all comes back.
    And the winter-time is here!
    Wow! Hear me howl!

For Olive and June and white Irene,
And the Mexican Kid and little Corinne:
Daughters of joy who have not been seen
    This many and many a year!
I'm a lone old wolf and I've lost my pack,
    And the winter time is here!
    Wow! Hear me howl!

Lonesome Bar

Forty

I.

Billy, I seem this late October day
  To hear the toll of some dull-throated bell!
They're calling time on me, and the game's to play:
  But what the hell, Bill—what the hell!

II.

Let me alone awhile! I want to stay
  Unanxious for an hour o'er what's ahead:
I'll make no vow at forty; this birthday
  We'll give to memories of the Past instead.

III.

Turn back thirty years! Sit down and try
  To call the times we had, the things we said,
The fresh sweet taste of life so long gone by,
  When you and I and Dick, and others dead,

IV.

Made great romance beneath a Western sky,
  Living thro' all the Seasons presently:
Then was no Past, and for the Future—why
  That was a treasure-cave of things to be.

V.

Now you have won a name and places high,
  And little Dick has grown so great and grey:
The luckier ones are seen no more, while I
  Go wandering an unprofitable way.

VI.

Last year, at Ottawa, I mind Noël,
  After each story that you told, would say,

YOUTH/OLD

Drinking old brandy in that old hotel,
  "La vie est triste, mon brave—soyons gai!"

VII.

And that's a song for all, when all is said:
  Billy, I'd like to be in some café
With some of those choice fellows that you've led
  And put a purple finish to this day.

VIII.

Tho' I'm no inky pessimist, nor bred,
  When I am hurt, to howl against the sky,
Yet there be times I turn a troubled head,
  And for one hour of rich abandon sigh.

IX.

But let it go! To all I've had to say
  Hear that dull-throated bell make one reply!
Half-time is call'd for me, and the game's to play,
  And still I've made no score—no score—yet I

X.

Have many dreams like jewels hid away,
  And many love me—more than I can tell:
And my heart is warm to all my friends this day,—
  So what the hell, Bill—what the hell!

Lonesome Bar

Ballade of the Easy Way

God I think is a balancer,
  And runs the World by compromise:
From brief observing I infer
  His line of least resistance lies
  Curving smoothly thro' the skies,
Forever mixing night and day,
  With all that such a thing implies:
Myself, I go the easy way.

'Tis a good thing at times to fight:
  To give a blow, and take a blow,
And hand it back with gathered might:
  'Tis the bully plan of the World below:
  And yet somehow as we older grow
We're not so keen for every fray:
  We'd liefer miss than meet a foe:
Myself, I go the easy way.

Troubles a-plenty we may not pass:
  Tangles too many we cannot untie:
And there's a pitiful end for us all, alas!
  But we can slip round so much, if we try,
  Or stay things off till by and by
We find they mostly are off to stay.
  Or matter no more at all: that's why
Myself, I go the easy way.

And the value of laughter, the value of tears,
  And the meaning of Life may be as it may:
In the bitter-sweet wisdom of later years
  Myself, I go the easy way.

Rhymes of a Rounder

YOUTH/OLD

The Ballad of Youth Remaining

Pardon if I ravel rhyme
   Out of my head disorderly!
Forgetting how the rats of time
   Are nibbling at the bones of me!
   But while upon my legs I'm free
Out in the sunlight I intend
   To dine with God prodigiously:
Youth is a splendid thing to spend!

Here's to the man who travels still
   In the light of young discoveries!
Here's to the fellow of lusty will,
   Who drives along and hardly sees
   For glamor of great realities
The doom of age! This line I send
   To all who sing hot litanies:
Youth is a splendid thing to spend!

But 'tis not all a matter of years:
   'Tis a way of living handily
In a game with Life, while yet appears
   A glory near of victory;
   With ventures high, and gallantry
Twinkling 'round the nearest bend
   Where damsels and fine dangers be:
Youth is a splendid thing to spend!

Fellows, come and ride with me
   Swiftly now to the edge of the end,
Holding the Stars of Joy in fee!—
   Youth is a splendid thing to spend!

Rhymes of a Rounder

Villanelle of Mutton

Very sick and tired I am
  Of stewed prunes, and apples dried,
And this our mutton that once was lamb!

I will make no grand salaam
  For the stale cakes the gods provide!
Very sick and tired I am!

My indignant diaphragm
  Would cover something fresh, untried,—
Not this mutton that once was lamb!

How every verse and epigram
  Of hope the lagging years deride!
Very sick and tired I am!

Must I always then be calm,
  And talk as one quite satisfied
With this our mutton that once was lamb?

Frankly, I don't give a dam
  For taste of things too long denied!
Very sick and tired I am
Of this our mutton that once was lamb!

Rhymes of a Rounder

Ballade of Sleep

I've lost my taste for things somehow
   That on a time were very sweet:
Sin has no savor for me now,—
   I find no apples good to eat:
   You laugh, and say that I'm effete,
But you are on the way, my friend,
   And after me you'll soon repeat:
Sleep is the best thing in the end.

Yet I come not with sour intent
   Against my old desires to prate:
Truly I do not repent,
   I only wish I knew some great
   Exultant vice to stimulate
What spark of Life remains to spend:
   But this I feel, as the hour grows late,
Sleep is the best thing in the end.

All things wear out, so much we see:
   All things must fall without reprieve:
Yet spite of that invincibly
   Upon the brink I still believe
   That God has hidden up his sleeve
For us some golden dividend:
   What think you then we shall receive?
Sleep is the best thing in the end.

Brother, down on a soundless bed
   From the ways of pain may we descend!
The stars creep dimly overhead:—
   Sleep is the best thing in the end.

Rhymes of a Rounder

E. EARTHLY CONSIDERATIONS

EARTHLY CONSIDERATIONS

Ballade of Detachment

The Lords of Karma deal the cards,
   But the game we play in our own way:
Now as for me, and as regards
   The gain or loss from day to day,
   I go detached; I mean to say
That I live largely as I please,
   Whether it does or does not pay
Among the inequalities.

With duties not too much engrossed,
   With profits not too much concerned,
Not to glean to the uttermost,
   Nor grieve for what I might have earned,
   This for my soul's sake I have learned,
Reaching for sweeter things than these:
   Pennies and fractions I have spurned
Among the inequalities.

O, damnable palavering
   Of pedagogues too regular!
I'd rather be a tramp, or sing
   For my living at a bar,
   Or peddle peanuts, far by far,
Than lose my reasonable ease
   In tow of rule and calendar
Among the inequalities.

Content if I may go a bit
   In my own way before I cease;
Living trimly by my wit
   Among the inequalities.

Rhymes of a Rounder

The Tiger of Desire
Villanelle

Starving, savage, I aspire
  To the red meat of all the World:
I am the Tiger of Desire!

With teeth bared, and claws uncurled,
  By leave o' God I creep to slay
The innocent of all the World.

Out of the yellow, glaring day,
  When I glut my appetite,
To my lair I slink away.

But in the black, returning night
  I leap resistless on my prey,
Mad with agony and fright.

The quick flesh I tear away,
  Writhing till the blood is hurled
On leaf and flower and sodden clay.

My teeth are bared, my claws uncurled,
  Of the red meat I never tire;
In the black jungle of the World
  I am the Tiger of Desire!

Rhymes of a Rounder

The Modernists

How very modern once they were
    In Nineveh and Babylon—
Maybe earlier in Ur!

Arrantly they play upon
    A single string to make a tune—
Declaring it the paragon!

Youngsters of the New Moon,
    With bubble ponderosity
Would pin a permanent on Noon!

Witless of how brief may be
    The consummated, smart, elated
Click of their modernity!

Or late or soon evaluated,
    Fine Art is of no epoch drawn,
And Beauty's like the sky-undated!

Now they're here and now they're gone!
    How very modern once they were
In Nineveh and Babylon—
    Maybe earlier in Ur!

In the Old of My Age

Dreamers in Romance

Dreamers in romance prefer obscure
Coverage to brash publicity:
Rose enamoured memories endure
Across the drift of years more pleasantly
Than any flashback into gross desire
Followed in swarmy streets where men compete,
Or offices where profiteers conspire.
Lucky they be who by themselves retreat
Beyond their heaviness to realize,
Thro' one or many of its many ways,
Romance arriving with some new surprise
To rich the gliding hours of nights and days!
    Grin, you worldly wise—or look askance—
    I tag along with dreamers in romance!

In the Old of My Age

Always Trouble
Cantel

Always trouble here:
Always trouble to fear:
    On from Eocene till now
Around this bloody sphere.

Who can disallow
The everlasting row
    Of carnal creatures that appear
From primal urge somehow?

Yet with so much to fear,
And trouble always near,
    So many do so well I vow
God himself should cheer!

In the Old of My Age

EARTHLY CONSIDERATIONS

What Answer?

Captain-Captain come from the wars—
    You with your arm in a sling—
Tell me, did you see my boy!
    Tell me everything!

God shield you now from pain, Lady!
    God ease your heart in sorrow!
The sky is so red in the west I think
    We'll have a fine day tomorrow!

But Captain-Captain come from the wars—
    Tell me—tell me true—
What did you see of my boy out there,
    Fighting along with you?

God shield you from pain, Lady!
    God ease your heart in sorrow!
The sky is so red in the west I think
    We'll have a fine day tomorrow!

Captain—how does the battle go?
    And when will come the end?
And when will my boy come back to me?
    What message did he send?

God shield you from pain, Lady!
    God ease your heart in sorrow!
The sky is so red in the west I think
    We'll have a fine day tomorrow!

In the Old of My Age

The Master Profiteers

Wanting more from masses having less,
The Master Profiteers continually
Scheme for gain regardless of distress—
Playing to counterpoint of scarcity!
Come war, come peace, come further world disquiet,
Ample still they hoard to serve their own,
Tho' millions must endure on famine diet
The while they gather for themselves at alone!
Gleefully they put their plans across—
Manipulator of financial trust,
Captain of cartel, or labour boss—
God, how they reek alive of money lust,
    Castled in luxury unknown before,
    With their gimme women wanting more!

In the Old of My Age

Plotted Not for Profit

Its own beatitude beyond belief
    Accrues of genial dealing everywhere:
    Openly or covert, here and there
Around this wrangling world we find one chief
Reason for unnecessary grief
    Comes those demanding more than fair—
    Comes if grabbing for the biggest share:
I wonder why—when having is so brief!
Relieving pain; providing proper food
    For hungry ones, regardless of their creed;
    Aiding others freely in their need—
Angels applaud each generous interlude
    Plotted not for profit! Clean of greed,
Its beauty is its own beatitude!

In the Old of My Age

The Odd Impulse to Serve

The odd impulse to serve that now has come
    Breaking thro' my crusted selfishness,
    Imports no ideology I guess—
I rise for no totalitarian drum!
Goodwill for good; more than that for some;
    And sign me on for local helpfulness!
    But I've no plan to lift beyond distress,
Or abrogate forever every slum!
I'm dim of vision, and I lack the nerve
    To formulate a fabulous revealing:
    Yet still remains persistently the feeling
Of finer reaches maybe round this curve—
    The curtain of my ignorance concealing
Splendour of the odd impulse to serve!

In the Old of My Age

F. LOVE AND OTHER PLEASURES

Mirelle of Found Money

I got a thousand dollars to-day
  By chance and undeservedly:
But nary a one of my debts will I pay:
  Sure it never was meant to be spent that way:
'Tis a gift from my fairy godmother, you see.

Except, of course, to my landlady,
  And some on account to the tailor Malone:
And there'll be a new dress, and a hat maybe,
For the lame girl who is good to me:
  But the rest of these dollars are all my own.

A thousand dollars and all for my own:
  The thought of it runs like a tune through my head:
So long it is since I have known
One lavish hour, one fully blown
  Rose of joy unheralded!

Tho' we of the world must grind for bread
  'Tis a plan I hold in small esteem:
And while I can taste I let no dread
Of later want contract the spread
  Of my desire for cakes and cream.

Wrapt in myself, obscure, supreme,
  I slip thro' streets and quarters gay,
And the comic crowd I see in a dream,
But glory be—this is no dream:
  I got a thousand dollars to-day!

Rhymes of a Rounder

Mirelle of the Good Bed

There's nothing so good as a good bed
   When a body is over and done with day!
I'd like a place to lay my head
   In a clean room, unfrequented
And dark, unless for a moon-ray.

O, Angel of Dreams, without delay
   Then let me from this World be gone!
Within a temple I would pray
   Where golden odors float alway
Onward to oblivion.

Or haply may I be withdrawn
   From pain and care and manners mean
Into some fairy tower whereon
The glim, bejewelled gonfalon
   Of blue enchantery is seen!

But a lady I know might come between
   Laughing, and lead me far astray
On the flowery edge of a wild ravine
Where wild cascades of waters green
   Flash in the pleasant light of May.

Thus let me dream the night away,
   Or slumber dreamless with the dead!
Life may resume, but now I say,
Being too weary of the day,
   There's nothing so good as a good bed!

Rhymes of a Rounder

Love

Love will ever find a way
To turn the darkest night to day:
Out of chaos and mischance,
And every wicked circumstance,
'Twill build itself a home again
Within the hearts of erring men;
But hell is made by its inhabitants.

The Fool of Joy

Among the Queers
Cantel

Sometimes among the queers,
When passion disappears,
    Love puts velvet in between
The wearing of the years.

Urgency and green
Delight of youth get lean
    Soon or late, as ending nears
And sorrows intervene.

Yet among the queers,
Age sometimes endears,
    And love puts velvet in between
The wearing of the years.

In the Old of My Age

Zalinka

1

Last night in a land of triangles,
  I lay in a cubicle, where
A girl in pyjamas and bangles
  Slept with her hands in my hair.

2

I wondered if either or neither
  Of us were properly there,
Being subject to queer aberrations—
Astral and thin aberrations—
  Which leave me no base to compare:
  No adequate base to compare:
But her hands, with their wristful of bangles,
  Were certainly fast in my hair,
While the moon made pallid equations
  Thro' a delicate window there.

3

I was glad that she slept for I never
  Can tell what the finish will be:
What enamoured, nocturnal endeavor
  May end in the killing of me:
But, in the moonlit obscure
  Of that silken, somniferous lair,
Like a poet consumed with a far lust
  Of things unapproachably fair
I fancied her body of stardust—
Pounded of spices and stardust—
  Out of the opulent air.

4

Then the moon, with its pale liquidations,
  Fell across her in argentine bars,

And I thought: This is fine—but to-morrow
   What cut of Dawn's cold scimitars
Will sever my hold on this creature—
   I mean of this creature on me?
Amorous creature of exquisite aura—
   Marvel of dark glamorie.

5

What joy of folly then followed
   Is beyond my expression in rhyme:
And I do not expect you to grasp it
   When I speak of expansions of time:
Of reaching and zooming serenely
   As it were at right angles to time:
Knowing well you will think, on your level,
   This was only a dream indiscreet—
   Or experience quite indiscreet:
But little I care, in this instance,
   What you do or do not think discreet:
   O utterance futile, but sweet,
   Like a parrot I pause and repeat,
In delight of my own, and for nothing,
   To myself I repeat and repeat:

6

Last night in a land of triangles,
   I lay in a cubicle where
A girl in pyjamas and bangles
   Slept with her hands in my hair.

Roundabout Rhymes

G. NATURE

NATURE

Yolana

1

There's a by-road the saints fear,
   And the wizards seek in vain;
Ayont the day 'tis quite near,
Yet the way of it is too queer
   For me to make it plain;
But we find our track by the Zodiac,
   Then a body parts in twain,
And we be lift in a mode to the mere
   Mass a madness vain,
   A dream or delusion vain.
    Yolana avie avie avie!
      Yolana vekana vor!

2

But what and O! what may the mass know
   Of the things that are done of us?
On the round hill where we go
To bide our time in the pale glow
   For Yolana marvellous?
And visions evoke by sweet smoke
   And breathings tremulous?
Nay, the sound of words may not show
   The things that are done of us—
   Remotely done of us!
    Yolana avie avie avie!
      Yolana vekana vor!

3

A gold star in the West glow'd
   Thro' a night obscurely clear;
'Twas the dry time when the winds bode
Thro' the treetops, and the tree toad
   Answers eerily;

The dwarf came with the swart name
  A-whispering in my ear;
And I nodded and took the by-road
  Thro' the night obscurely clear
  As a smoky-topaz is clear.
    Yolana avie avie avie!
      Yolana vekana vor!

4

Where the lone pine tree flings
  A ragged shadow down
We light the fire, and the dwarf sings
To keep away the bad things
  That glimmer about and frown,
As we mix the wine and make the sign
  They made in the sunken town:—
Then O! a glory of light wings
  Bearing Yolana down!
    Yolana avie avie avie!
      Yolana vekana vor!

5

But what and O! what may the mass know
  Of the things that are done of us?
On the round hill where we go
To slumber in the pale glow
  Of planets pendulous?
And out of the skies materialize
  Yolana marvellous?
Nay, the sound of words may not show
  The things that are done of us—
  Remotely done of us!
    Yolana avie avie avie!
      Yolana vekana vor!

6

O the twinkling stones of faëry
   When Yolana comes!
 All set in the greenest jewelry,
  While the magic smoke goes bluely
   From the burning magic gums!
 And we troll the chants in a ghost-dance
   To the monotone of drums,
 Till we lapse for sheer enchantery
   When Yolana comes!
    Yolana avie avie avie!
    Yolana vekana vor!

Lonesome Bar

Indian Summer Beauty
Cantel

September! Fragrant—fruity
Still of ripe and rooty
   Harvest largely gathered clean
Of superfluity!

Blue clearings thro' the green
In the woods are seen,
   With autumn-come annuity
Of gold and grenadine.

Happily off duty,
I ramble for the booty
   Had by those who love the Queen
Of Indian Summer Beauty.

In the Old of My Age

Good-Bye
Villanelle

All things are reapt beneath the sky,
   And I'll be gone before the year:
Girl, in October we say good-bye!

Remember how the May was mere
   With white and green and violet!
Remember all that followed, dear!

How June, with wreath and coronet
   Of many roses amorous
Led us dreaming deeper yet!

Thro' red July victorious
   To August, ample, passionate!
No lovers e'er had more than us.

Now bronze September soon will set:
   I want no life extended drear
Till Youth and Summer we forget.

O Autumn, haunted, sweet and sere!
   All things are reapt beneath the sky!
And I'll be gone before the year:
   Girl, in October we say good-bye!

Rhymes of a Rounder

H. DEATH

DEATH

The Tomb

And he is dead at last! O long ago—
   So long ago it is since yesterday!
   The World hath sunken round me, old and grey,
To sound of endless litanies of woe:—
Dear God, if I could know—could only know
   Beyond the creeds and feeble prayers they say
   That I might find him yet in some sure way—
How I would laugh against this Tomb below!

I've lost the meaning of the words he said
   To ease my heart before he pass'd from me:
   I walk the ruin'd Earth in agony,
And cry unto the Waste uncomforted:
   Across the blacken'd Skies I start to see
His name writ flamingly—but he is dead!

A Romance of the Lost

The Isles of Gold
Cantel

Away from days too cold,
Away from hearts too old,
   Honey-Mouth, O Honey-Mouth,
I go to the Isles of Gold!

Will it be to North or South
That I find them, Honey-Mouth?
   The King no entry there I'm told
Except the dead alloweth!

So be it, from days too cold!
So be it, from hearts too old!
   Honey-Mouth, O Honey-Mouth,
I go to the Isles of Gold!

Rhymes of a Rounder

DEATH

Ballade of Waiting

There was a time that Death for me
   Unbalanced every new delight:
Its cold, abhorrent mystery
   Haunted me by day and night:
   I felt its noisome, clammy blight
Making of life a mildewed thing:
   But now to its face I cry: Alright!
I'm no afraid for the outgoing!

Because so many I loved have gone
   I stare a-wondering at the skies:
The World below I look upon
   With listless, old, exhausted eyes:
   The while for every friend who dies
I feel a queerish loosening
   Within of all familiar ties:
I'm no afraid for the outgoing!

I weary under a weight of days,
   Withering and too sensible
Of aged needs and altered ways:
   But this one thing is good to tell:
   In the wintry desert where I dwell
Some rumor I have heard of spring,
   And I have dreamed of asphodel:
I'm no afraid of the outgoing!

The sweet renewal of the air,
   And the call of Youth recovering—
Do these await me yet somewhere?
   I'm no afraid of the outgoing!

Rhymes of a Rounder

With the Seven Sleepers
Cantel

O fairy, take me far
To some enchanted star!
   Let me go sleep for a thousand years
Where the Seven Sleepers are!

Beyond the striving spheres,
Beyond all hopes or fears,
   Where never a black or golden bar
Of Hell or Heaven appears!

O Fairy, take me far
Away from things that are!
   Let me go sleep for a thousand years
In some enchanted star!

Rhymes of a Rounder

DEATH

Ballade of the Picaroon

I knew him for a picaroon
  Among the purlieus of the town:
At free lunch in a beer saloon
  To wash the cheese and pickles down,
  With pretzels hard and salt and brown,
We drank and talked of all our schemes
  To banish Fortune's chronic frown:
He was a fine fellow of dreams.

He loved the light, piquant details
  Of life beyond mere livelihood;
And while he covered many trails
  More tricks he played and girls he wooed
  And bottles emptied than he should
For that success the World esteems:
  But after a fashion he made good:
He was a fine fellow of dreams.

Because I heard his death to-night
  Told in the hotel corridor
I left the crowd for the cool starlight
  And the lone ways: my heart was sore
  That I should see his face no more
Where the wheel turns, and the light gleams.
  And the air reels to the World's uproar:
He was a fine fellow of dreams.

My friend he was and he died too soon:
  'Tis always too soon for his like it seems:
But he lived while he lived, that picaroon—
  He was a fine fellow of dreams.

Rhymes of a Rounder

ANTHOLOGY

Wan Angel over Me
Cantel

Wan Angel over me,
Stoop low and loose me free
   Away from these my faltering years,
And mean infirmity!

I've no phantom fears
As my dying nears,
   Yet still it grieves me bitterly
For some I brought to tears!

Stoop low and loose me free
From clutch of Memory—
   Clear me away to new-born years—
Wan Angel over me!

In the Old of My Age

Wondrous Anodyne!

Wondrous anodyne the Angel brings!
   So darkly with ease and quietude!
   Pains obliterate, and all the rude
Reminders of old griefs and wrongdoings
Drift away among forgotten things!
   I would relax now in oblivious mood,
   And from my long itinerant conclude:
My life to form of life no longer clings!
I'd be quit now of what's me for mine—
   Troubling with outworn material:
   I'd dream into surcease beyond the real—
Entering a somnolence divine:
   O lovely twilight deepening over all—
Oh perfect peace! Oh wondrous anodyne!

In the Old of My Age

I. RELIGION

Content

But God stays—tho' all else fail and fall!
  He seems sometimes a Playfellow of mine
  Who winks at me and laughs—sometimes a fine,
Red Flame to gloriously destroy: a Call
To bring green Worlds again: immemoral
  A Mood that wakes in me: an Anodyne
  To soothe me unto Death: a Sound divine:
A dim enamour'd Silence under all.

Amid the jar of things, and in wrong ways,
  I hurt myself continually, and yet
  Withal I stand, and with fix'd eyes forget
The bitter unfulfilment of my days,
  And feel my way to Him, content to let
All else between my fingers slip—God stays!

A Romance of the Lost

Nirvana

Down the ages comes a sound grown dark
   With unremember'd meaning. Many heard
   Fall from the lips of One illum'd a word
Whose doubtful gospel seem'd to quench all spark
Of separate love and joy, with promise stark,
   If from their patient hearts still undeterr'd
   They rooted all desire—the boon conferr'd
Should be to pass from Life without a mark.

Old devotees, dream on! Old scholars nod
   Over the meaning of the Indian sage!
   But I, awakening in a later age,
Choose not the deserts where His saints have trod,
   Nor cleave to ancient rites or holy page;
Singing on my careless way to God.

A Romance of the Lost

RELIGION

The Gentle Knave
Cantel

The knave had gathered much odd
And singular knowledge abroad
   Regarding all flowers that are under the sun,
And bones that are under the sod.

The end of his life had begun,
And he felt that his travels were done,
   But he smiled in finding the asphodel nod
At the root of minus one.

Then he willed his bones to the sod,
And his flowers to the fields that he trod,
   And he bowed at the root of minus one
To the wind that is older than God.

Roundabout Rhymes

Infidel

Believe as I believe, or go to Hell!
   Thus always bigots would bedevil us
   With ideologies contrarious!
They'd force us all to be comfortable
Exclusively to their conclusions! Well,
   Glory be I'm still obstreperous,
   And 'gainst the crush of creeds incredulous!
That goes for Science too—I'm Infidel!
I stay myself—let physicos conceive
   Me but the passing function of a gland!
   I know me more! Tho' if we lend a hand
Some misery immediate to relieve,
   I'll be no missionary to demand
That every man believe as I believe!

In the Old of My Age

BIBLIOGRAPHY

• FOSTER, Hamar. "A Romance of the Lost: The Role of Tom MacInnes in the History of the British Columbia Indian Land Question" in *Essays in the History of Canadian Law*, University of Toronto Press, 2016, p. 171–212.

• DEACON, William Arthur. *A Canadian Literary Life*, University of Toronto Press, 1982.

• GLYNN-WARD, Hilda. *The Writing on the Wall*, University of Toronto Press, 2010.

• MACINNES, Tom. *For the Crowning of the King*, Evans & Hastings, 1902

• MACINNES, Tom. *A Romance of the Lost*, Desbarats & Co., 1908.

• MACINNES, Tom. *Lonesome Bar*, Desbarats & Co., 1909.

• MACINNES, Tom. *In Amber Lands*, Broadway Publishing, 1910.

• MACINNES, Tom. *Rhymes of a Rounder*, Broadway Publishing, 1913.

• MACINNES, Tom. *The Fool of Joy*, McClelland, Goodchild & Stewart Publishers, 1918.

• MACINNES, Tom. *Roundabout Rhymes*, The Ryerson Press, 1923.

• MACINNES, Tom. *The Complete Poems of Tom MacInnes*, The Ryerson Press, 1923.

• MACINNES, Tom. *Chinook Days*, Sun Publishing Co. Ltd, 1926.

• MACINNES, Tom. *Oriental Occupation of British Columbia*, Sun Publishing, Vancouver, 1927.

- MACINNES, Tom. *High Low Along: A Didactic Poem*, Clarke & Stuart, 1934.
- MACINNES, Tom. *In the Old of My Age*, The Ryerson Press, 1947.
- POUND, Ezra. *ABC of Reading*, Routledge, 1934.
- RHODENIZER, V. B. *Handbook of Canadian Literature*, Graphic Publishers, 1931.
- ROBIN, Martin. *Shades of Right: Nativist and Fascist Politics in Canada, 1920-1940*, University Press, 1992.
- Unknown. *The Vancouver Poetry Society, 1918-1946*, The Ryerson Press, 1946.
- WARD, W. Peter. *White Canada Forever*, McGill-Queen's University Press, 2002.
- WOODCOCK, George. *British Columbia, A History of the Province*, Douglas & McIntyre Ltd, 1990.

© 2021 Reconquista Press
www.reconquistapress.com